YOU CAN SAIL

YOU CAN SAIL

by John R. Whiting

Photographs by
Peter Barlow and Stanley Rosenfeld

Foreword by Rod Stephens

Illustrations by Philip Wright

 HEARST BOOKS

NEW YORK

Library of Congress Cataloging in Publication Data

Whiting, John R.
   You can sail.

   Includes index.
   1. Sailing. I. Title.
GV811.W49   797.1'24   81-4281
ISBN 0-87851-806-1   AACR2
ISBN 0-87851-807-X (pbk.)

Hearst Books
224 West 57 street
New York, N.Y. 10019
Printed in the U.S.A.

Book design by John R. Whiting and Arlene Goldberg

Acknowledgments

Arlene Goldberg for her design contributions; Jack Howie, Nick James, and Julien Davies, Howmar Boats, Inc., Edison, N.J.; Roy M. Hutchins and Karen Taylor, sailors of the boat photographed for the cover; Dave Hartman, Shirley Hartman, Shelley LeClerc, Bob LeClerc, and Manuel Blanco, sailors of the boat shown in Chapters 2, 3, and 4; Sohei Hohri, librarian of the New York Yacht Club; Queene Hooper for invaluable research assistance, fact-checking, and editing the glossary; Robert Ogg for his contributions to the art of anchoring.

Peter Barlow made the pictures on pages 10 through 29, and 72, 74-75, 77, 100,113,116,122,123,125 and the frontispiece.

Stanley Rosenfeld made the pictures on pages 30 through 71, and 76, 78, 79, 80 and 112.

Dedication

To Ruth Smith McCann, from whom I learned
much about excellence in publishing—
as she learned it from Charles F. Chapman.

CONTENTS

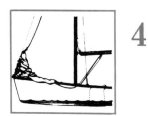

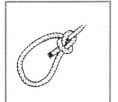

FOREWORD

Sailing turns some people off; they believe that it's just too complicated, and that it would take them too long to reach the point of enjoyment. But as John Whiting so clearly brings out in this book, if you are really interested in sailing and really want to learn how, learning becomes quick and easy. The important thing is to have a good teacher—a sailor, or a book written by a sailor—who keeps things simple, and who explains enough as he goes along so that you can understand it, but avoids making things so complex that you get discouraged. You'll soon realize that one of the fascinations of sailing is that anyone who is deeply interested in it will continue to learn as long as he sails, for, after all, no one ever really knows all there is to know about sailing. That just makes the enjoyment all the greater!

So don't be turned off by those who try to make sailing too complex. The title of this book tells the true story: *you can sail*. Just take it step by step, with care. Let me add two of the briefest but best instructions I received in the early days of my own sailing: "Continual learning is the nature of sailing," and "Eternal vigilance is the price of safety."

—Roderick Stephens, Jr.

Participation in a sail training program, such as this one in Connecticut, offers novices on-the-water practice.

INTRODUCTION

When you're learning to sail, there's no substitute for the feel of the wind on your face, the motion of the waves and the boat, and the sounds of sails and rigging singing in your ear. That's why this book encourages you to get out on the water as soon as possible. At the same time, there's no substitute for knowing what you're doing. That's why you're reading this book.

The basic steps in learning to sail have been carefully simplified in this manual. And we've adopted the best course for beginners to follow: a step-by-step approach. Read

Learning to sail aboard an old but graceful catboat has its own nostalgic magic.

through the first procedures and then get out on the water and try them; when you've mastered the first steps, read some more, and then go out and improve your skills with further practice.

Here's a happy thought: you probably know a great deal about sailing already. You may have been around the waterfront and may recognize boats and much of their anatomy. Or you may know about knots, bends, and hitches even before you go out. Perhaps you have picked up a facility for forecasting the weather. Or you have been sailing with friends and "almost know how." This book was written for you and others who need to fill in the gaps. Of course, if you learn sailing with a partner, you'll pool your bits of knowledge, and progress that much faster.

Three basic assumptions have been made in this book:

First, you'll start learning on a particular type of boat. For the first few teaching chapters, all the illustrations and descriptions refer to a specific boat, the Designer's Choice. She is just under 15 feet long and sloop-rigged, that is, she has one mast and carries a mainsail and a jib. She has built-in flotation, which makes her a good family boat. She was intended for teaching purposes, but she can race, too. Actually your boat may be a small cat-rigged dinghy or your uncle's cruising yawl, but since the basic anatomy of most small boats is much the same, our choice has been Designer's Choice. You'll find scores of similar boats with similar rigging all over the world.

Second, you can learn to sail properly and safely in a very short time. It's the nature of sailing that anyone can pick up the basics quickly and easily but that the serious sailor goes on learning for decades. Thus, this book doesn't try to tell you everything at once; the important skills are explained first, and some fine points and options are saved for later chapters. We've tried to avoid arguable points and subjects that require elaborate explanations altogether.

And third, the language of sailing is part of the fun. It may be possible to teach sailing without using the nautical vocabulary, but that would really be the hard way. There are so many objects and situations found only on the water that sailors have had to create their own language. What we've tried to do is explain the meaning of special terms the first time they're used. If you spend any time around boats, you'll soon learn how to use these terms naturally and see how easy they make it for sailors to talk with one another. At the end of the book there is a glossary of the basic sailing terms used, with concise definitions.

Different people bring different points of view to this learning process. If you're the owner of a boat or plan to be one, your attitude should be basically one of responsibility. You will decide whether or not to sail on a day that might be too windy for beginners. You're responsible for the maintenance of the boat. It's your job to see that the proper equipment is on board every time you go out. On the other hand, if you're learning to sail in order to crew on someone else's boat, then your attitude should be one of cooperation. If you make yourself a skillful and reliable helper, you'll be invited more often.

Although you'll acquire the basic skills quickly enough, don't get overconfident. At first, go out only when the wind is light to moderate. Don't attempt difficult maneuvers such as sailing up to a dock until you can handle the boat with ease. You can learn as much by watching how other boats and other sailors behave as by keeping your eye on the details of your own craft.

Sailing is a safe sport. It's safe statistically and it's safe for anyone who sails correctly. Here are three safety standards that beginners ignore at their peril:

▲ Don't go sailing when you cannot deal competently with wind and water conditions. If your experience isn't sufficient to warn you clearly about this, don't hesitate to ask an experienced sailor for advice. After you become more proficient, you'll be able to sail in conditions that keep beginners ashore.

▲ Inspect the rigging and sails of your boat frequently to see if they're set up properly, to learn how they behave under different conditions, and to spot wear and damage before they become serious. Don't attempt maneuvers in the water that your boat isn't designed or equipped to do.

▲ Be sure the proper safety gear is on board every time out. This means you *must* have personal flotation devices for every person aboard as required by government regulations and you *must* be able to make the emergency signals specified in the regulations.

Safe sailing also means learning things by hearsay and not from unhappy experience. Dress properly. Getting a bad sunburn on the water is an easy mistake to make; getting uncomfortably cold when afternoon shadows lengthen is another. Sailing barefoot looks like fun, but when you cut your foot on a sharp cleat, you'll learn that nonskid deck shoes are a better way to go. Most knowledgeable sailors do not permit barefoot sailing on their boats.

Can you get lost on the water? Of course you can—if you haven't learned how to keep track of where you are, if you aren't aware that a fog bank can creep up on little cat feet, and if you haven't learned how to sail at night. Acquire the skills you need to deal with these situations early. And if you sail where there are miles and miles of open water, be sure you learn elementary piloting.

You'll never exceed the speed limit in a sailboat, and you'll rarely endanger other boats, but there are police boats in many localities whose job is to restrain motorboats engaged in high jinks and to help people in trouble. You may occasionally see Coast Guard boats doing the same jobs.

One of the special things about boating is the attitude of helpfulness that most sailors show to one another. Some day when you're becalmed and tired of waiting for the wind to pick up, you'll be grateful when you're offered a tow home. You can pay back that favor by helping someone else when the opportunity comes your way. There is also a gratifying number of volunteer helpers on the water. The U.S. Power Squadrons (their members usually fly their special ensign) and the U.S. Coast Guard Auxiliary provide free boating education. Other countries have similar volunteer educational organizations.

The variety of sailboat designs is tremendous. They have evolved to meet sailing conditions on many different kinds of water—oceans, lakes, bays, even rivers. When you decide to buy a boat, it's a good idea to get one that's similar to the most popular type you find on the waters you'll be sailing on.

If you learn to sail in a boat like the "teaching boat" shown in the first half of this book, you'll find it easy to adapt to other boats, since the techniques that work best on a plain sloop transfer to most other rigs. (There are some execeptions, of course: this book doesn't deal with catamarans and other multihulled craft, nor with wind surfing—a separate athletic skill in itself.) And if your learning process occurs on a larger cruising boat, you'll certainly be able to sail a small boat with ease.

1

THE JOYS OF SAILING

You're up with the sun, poking your head out of the cabin and looking out over the quiet water of the harbor. The morning mist is still streaking white here and there as the first breeze scatters it. You watch a minute or two as the wind picks up fitfully. It's from the southwest, and that's as important a sign as the clear sky, slowly turning to blue: the day will be good for sailing.

Somewhere, not very near, a boat has slowly passed, and small rippling motions of the otherwise still water are reaching the hull of your boat. There's a hint of sound as the

wavelets lap against the topsides and a hint of rocking as the hull responds. It's one of the gentlest motions in the world, and the sound is music to a sailor's ear.

The warmth of the sun begins to reach you, and you know that the same warmth is also bringing the early morning breeze. Air over the slowly warming land is rising, and new air from seaward is pushing its way to replace it. Figures appear on the deck of a cruising boat anchored nearby. Silently they take off a sail cover and unfasten all but one of the white canvas ties that hold the furled sail snug atop the boom.

Watching two persons get a boat ready to sail has its own fascination. You hardly need

---

A quiet harbor, early in the morning, holds the promise of sailing pleasures.

It doesn't really matter at all whether you go anywhere or accomplish anything.

to know the names or functions of rigging items to follow the sequence of details. One of the figures looks aloft to make sure no lines are tangled or jammed; the halyard coming down from the masthead is snapped into the head of the mainsail as the pair prepares to hoist it. The line at the end of the boom near the stern, the sheet, is loosed, its coils checked to make sure they'll run free.

Another figure carries a sail bag forward; you watch him get the jib ready, fastening it on the wire jibstay and snapping the jib halyard into the upper corner of the sail so it can be raised.

Step by step, sheet by sheet, detail by detail, preparations are made. The sails go up, literally in a minute. The anchor comes in—almost the first noise you hear is the

A light touch on the tiller is all that is needed to keep the sails full.

rattle of a short length of chain—and the boat slowly starts to glide away, with one figure sitting at the tiller, steering with his fingertips. How effortless it seems when done by knowing and competent hands.

The skills used by those two sailors are universal. The procedures for setting sail would be almost the same anyplace in the world. The details might vary in colorful ways if you were watching a junk in Canton harbor, but the results would be precisely the same. There would be more rigging details if you were watching a schooner get under way. The job would be even simpler if it were a small dinghy with a single sail. But the wind would fill the sails in the same way, and the craft would heel to the wind gently and pick up speed with the same characteristic response.

It's even possible to entertain the fleet in a raft-up with a small concert.

As you look around the harbor with the other boats at their moorings, you know what the poet John Masefield meant by "sea fever," why there are a hundred ways to enjoy sailing, with not the least being the observation of other boats. The reflections in the water, the wheeling flight of sea birds that seem to sail in the air, the many kinds of boats—all are echoes of the many joys of sailing.

If you glance into the cabin, you may see a brass plate put there to express the love of the water with these words:

"Nice? It's the only thing," said the Water Rat solemnly, as he leant forward for his stroke. "Believe me, my young friend, there is nothing—absolutely nothing—half so much worth doing as simply messing about in boats. Simply messing about in boats—or with boats. In or out of 'em, it doesn't matter. Nothing seems really to matter, that's the

A sailboat is always surrounded by its own swimming pool—at least in warm waters.

charm of it. Whether you get away, or whether you don't; whether you arrive at your destination or whether you reach somewhere else, or whether you never get anywhere at all, you're always busy, and you never do anything in particular; and when you've done it there's always something else to do and you can do it if you'd like, but you'd much better not."

—Kenneth Grahame *The Wind in the Willows*

There are many other pleasures that Water Rat did not mention. For instance, the thrill of going fast; you don't go really fast, in fact, but it seems fast. There is satisfaction in the knowledge that it is your touch on the tiller, your adjustment of the sails, that makes the boat perk up when you want it to. It's neither muscle nor dial turning—it's skill.

Sailing a small boat is also good exercise, similar to the stretching and agile moving about of a dancer (not of a boxer or a football

Even a small boat with simple rigging can provide the thrill of sailing fast.

tackle), but you seldom think of the effort. You can be becalmed and go half asleep or be hard put to it on a windy day, and afterward find more restfulness in the cockpit than anywhere else in the world.

Even sailing people don't enjoy sitting for hours in a flat calm, or being cold and wet when the spray is flying. But they accept it as part of the game, and they know that tomorrow's beautiful sailing will make up for today's discomfort. Besides, touching hands with nature, even if the elements are not

An ocean-racing sloop heads out on her first Bermuda race.

always benign, is another constantly fascinating facet of boating.

The lore of sailing and the process of learning to sail are intertwined. Learning the special language, rich in history, contributes to the pleasure. Every part of a boat, from masthead to keel, has a specific name, and though it seems old-fashioned and unwieldy, the language a sailor uses to describe his boat and its behavior is extraordinarily precise. There are, for instance, at least a dozen different sails, each with its own name, in common use today; and there are perhaps twice as many types and rigs of boats. When you understand some of these words and

Two cruising sailboats, anchored in southern waters, enjoy a boating paradise.

learn four or five knots and a couple of simple mechanical skills, you've begun to acquire a new expertise.

You will then discover a kinship with Joshua Slocum, the first man to sail alone around the world, and perhaps even with a few clipper-ship captains. When the America's Cup trials and races are on, you will understand something of what the con-testants are up to, even if you have never set foot aboard a twelve-meter racing boat.

Of course, it's the actual sailing itself that's the special pleasure: learning to make your boat do what you want it to; gaining a sense of timing, a feeling for teamwork. Making a right-angle turn in an automobile doesn't take a crew trained to ten-second warnings and one-second actions, but aboard a sloop

that kind of teamwork is both necessary and satisfying.

Even slowing down and stopping are a special thing aboard a sailboat. You lower one sail and cut your speed in half. You head into the wind, just so, and as the boat stops, you drop anchor. There's more to it than parking a car, mainly because it is different each time; it's the knowledgeable planning of the ma-neuver that's the real skill and the real joy.

If you're a powerboating person (and that's another kind of fun), you discover that once you learn to handle a sailboat you become more expert at getting the powerboat away from a dock on a windy day. You also find you have a new kind of relaxation: sailing a dinghy around a snug harbor at sunset after you've anchored for the night.

For a sailor the love of one particular boat is usually important—and different from his feelings for other material objects. He can trade in high-fidelity equipment and take pride in the new—but he's not likely to hang on his wall a picture of the old amplifier and speakers. A sailor names his boat more imaginatively than any other possession, choosing among the names of stars in the heavens, heroines of history, names of storms or small breezes—or something whimsical.

You will always remember the first boat you sail and the first time you bump a dock, capsize a dinghy, or are briefly lost in a fog. You may be rueful, but eventually you will take pride in the way you surmounted the difficulty.

Before you become a sailor, such things as knots, bends, and hitches may seem a mystery, but if you tell yourself, "I can do that!" you'll find you can. When it comes to laying out a course on a chart, it seems easy when someone else does it, but a lot harder when you realize it may be dark when you finally get into harbor and you are responsible for finding the way. As you watch someone else bring a boat alongside another in the social maneuver known as rafting, you will notice the skill of the approach or the foolishness of not being prepared with the proper lines to tie up. You *do* cast a critical eye on your fellow sailor.

You may also cast a covetous eye on the other person's boat or way of doing things, but you'll soon discover something special about sailors: their willingness to share

A three-masted schooner, topsails and all, contrasts with a modern fiberglass sloop.

Rafting up, two or more boats at a time, is the sailor's way of getting together away from shore.

sources and ideas. This book shares a method for keeping the topping lift out of the roach of the mainsail, as demonstrated by Sam Barclay, a rigger at Yacht Haven in Connecticut. It illustrates the proper way to tie the throat of a sail bag, as practiced by sailmaker Dick Vallentine on City Island in New York. And it includes a quick and secure way to fasten a flagstaff to a flag halyard, which came from Eddie Quest, who is also from City Island.

Another pleasure of sailing is often enjoyed ashore in the off season. Old salts called it yarning, and it takes many forms. A friend may let you borrow his copy of *The Riddle of the Sands,* so that, at least in your

Once a few boats are safely rafted together, friends gather for a traditional on-board party.

mind's eye, you can go sailing in a tiny sloop along the Dutch and German coasts as they were before World War I. Or you may sit on the edge of a group talking about the Fastnet Race—any Fastnet Race, not just the one with the big storm—and somehow the rocky Scilly Isles will seem to be right there.

Whether you own a boat or sail with someone else, whether you take up the skills of piloting and navigation, whether you sail on a lake or a stormy ocean, the basic demands and pleasures of sailing are the same, and they are unique. Yet there are comparisons with other skills worth noting. Sailing is more like driving a trotting horse with a light sulky than like driving a car, and

Heading east on a cruise, two schooners with light sails set stand out against the summer sky.

has similarities with skiing. Not surprisingly, many airplane pilots like to sail. Both sailing and mountain climbing pit you against the elements, but because in sailing you are *using* the elements, there's a somewhat different sense of accomplishment. That is, when the elements don't get the better of you and rip a sail or give you a dousing.

In these pages you will meet different boats, learn their anatomies, and grow familiar with the language of sailing. You will also discover that a boat, with its sails, is really a simple machine for converting the wind's energy into motion, and you will get a feel of the need to control that process. These elements, together with the new things you'll learn to see and the harmonies you'll learn to hear, make up the many joys of sailing.

At day's end, if you've done your piloting accurately, you'll reach the buoy you intended.

2

INSTANT SAILING

You may have been sailing many times on a friend's boat. Or you may have been brought up far from the water, sailing in your imagination a hundred times as you read the Captain Horatio Hornblower stories or others about the sea. You may know the technical terms—or you may not. For now, let's say you're going out for a practice run around the bay, with a knowledgeable sailor guiding you through the first steps, helping you see, feel, and hear what's going on. This

In a light breeze a sloop sails close-hauled, with the wind coming from ahead and to the right (starboard). The sails are trimmed to balance each other and very little steering is needed.

person could be a sailing-school instructor, a helpful friend, or even the dealer who's selling you the boat.

The boat that you're going to learn to sail in this book is called Designer's Choice, a type of modern sloop about fifteen feet long. There are simpler and smaller boats and, of course, much larger cruising and ocean racing boats. But for mastering the rudiments, keeping gear to a useful minimum, and still having most of the advantages of learning aboard a boat with normal anatomy, the D-C, or a similar boat, is ideal.

In this first lesson let's concentrate on the basics: how to steer, how to sail with the wind coming from different directions, and how to

Sailing close-hauled. *The wind comes from ahead and to the side of the boat, and its pressure on the sails makes the boat move ahead.*

Sailing on a reach. *The wind is abeam, and the sails are let out to make a larger angle to the wind. The mainsail and jib are controlled by a mainsheet and jibsheet, respectively.*

change direction. For the moment, we'll let some of the details go: many nautical terms, names of equipment, how to get ready and get under way, and how to deal with strong winds, puffy winds, or no wind at all. These are all considered in later chapters; for now we're going sailing just to get the feel and a basic understanding of it. Let's call it "instant sailing."

Steering a straight course. The lesson begins when your instructor lets you take the tiller to steer the boat.

Let's say the wind is a light to moderate breeze, holding fairly constant. Simply hold the tiller steady, and learn to make corrections no larger than the width of your hand—this way you'll learn quickly enough

to sail a straight line. Now look ahead, line up part of the boat with a tree or a house on the shoreline across the bay, and steer toward it.

The tiller. The best way to learn how the tiller works is by trial and error. Push it to the right, or *starboard*, and the boat turns to the left, or *port*, and vice versa. A little logical observation shows how the tiller moves the rudder: since the rudder is mounted on a pivot, it moves in the direction *opposite* from the tiller. The force of the water against one side of the turned rudder pushes the stern, or back end, of the boat away, thus turning the bow, or front end, in the opposite direction. Push the tiller to starboard, and the bow points to port. Push the tiller to port and the bow comes round to starboard.

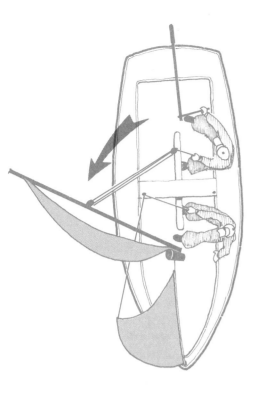 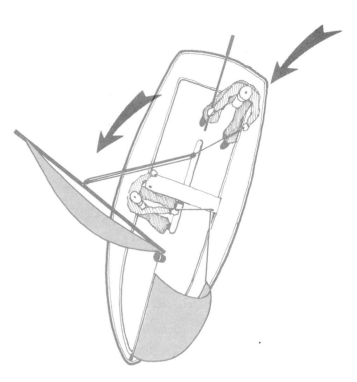

Running, or sailing downwind. *The wind is aft, and the mainsheet is eased far enough for the boom to be nearly at right angles to the wind. The jib is on the same side as the mainsail.*

Running wing and wing. *The boat sails directly before the wind, with the mainsail and jib on opposite sides; this requires a sure hand on the tiller and constant watchfulness.*

POINTS OF SAILING

Sailing on a reach. When the wind comes from one side, the boom is adjusted so that the mainsail angles out from the center of the boat away from the windward side. The jib— the forward sail—is at about the same angle: that is, partway out. The manner in which you're sailing—with the wind coming across the side at nearly right angles—is called *sailing on a reach.*

Reaching is the first of three *points of sailing* you'll learn in this lesson (point of sailing refers to the direction in which a boat is moving in relation to the direction of the wind). The wind is *abeam*, meaning it's at right angles to the boat's centerline when you're reaching.

Look at the drawing on page 32 that explains reaching. Notice the arrows showing wind direction. When the wind is apparently coming directly from the side, you are sailing on a *beam reach.* If you steer farther away from the wind, it's called a *broad reach*, and the sails are let out some. Conversely, if you

Sailing downwind in the normal way, the jib is on the same side as the mainsail. Here the wind is so light that the mainsheet isn't even taut.

point the boat more toward the wind and haul the sails in closer to the centerline, you're on a *close reach.* Thus there are three different degrees of reaching, but the changes from one to another are gradual.

Sailing downwind. Now let's try the second point of sailing, sailing *downwind,* or running, with the wind behind you. Move the tiller to the side the wind is coming from, and the boat will turn the other way—away from the wind, which will now be coming from behind. (The wind hasn't changed; you've changed the angle of the boat relative to the wind.) You are now sailing *downwind,* and the sails will be let out so they are more or less at right angles to the wind.

If you turn still farther away from the wind, the jib will flop over to the opposite side of the boat from the mainsail. This is called sailing *wing and wing* (see page 35), and it requires careful steering to keep the sails in that position. Better leave this technique until you become an experienced sailor.

Sailing downwind is so much quieter than reaching that you may think the wind has dropped. It hasn't, really, but because you're going in the same direction, the wind seems to be blowing more gently.

Throughout these maneuvers there has been a lot of talk about the wind. From the very beginning it is vital to grasp one cardinal rule of sailing: *Always know from what direction the wind is blowing.*

So far, you've been steering and finding out how different adjustments of the sails affect the movement of the boat. Most of all, you've been feeling different physical sensations. You can feel the boat heel from a puff of wind when you're on a close reach, and you can hear, by the quickening rhythm of small waves against the bow, just how the boat responds to such a puff with extra speed.

You're beginning to see why sailing is a skill. It is knowledge, and balance, and almost fingertip control of the tiller, not muscle power, that are important.

In a light wind you and your sailing partner can sit on opposite sides of the boat. But when you get on a close reach and the wind freshens a bit, it is best if you both sit on the high side to keep the boat from heeling over too far. You don't use muscle power, but you get plenty of exercise.

Sailing close-hauled. Now that you have the feeling of steering the boat, the sense of balance when the boat heels, and a little understanding of how she sails when reaching

Sailing downwind wing and wing, the jib is opposite the mainsail.

and running, it's time to try the third point of sailing, sailing *close-hauled*, or heading almost toward the wind.

The instructor hauls in the mainsheet, and then the jibsheet; under his instruction you steer the boat closer and closer to the wind, that is, closer to the direction from which the wind is coming. This is called sailing close-hauled, or sailing upwind, or sailing on the wind, or pointing—they all mean the same thing. Study the photograph on page 30 and the diagram on page 32 to familiarize yourself with the way it looks. With a little practice, you'll find that the boat will almost steer herself now. With a puff of wind she heels a little more and tends to head into the wind; you have to adjust for this by pulling the tiller a little toward the wind. If the wind slackens a bit, you ease the tiller back, and the boat adjusts and sails smoothly along.

Your sensations and perceptions while sailing close-hauled are worth remembering:

▲ The boat seems to be going fast.
▲ She heels more than she did before.
▲ The wind is almost in your face when you look forward.

Changing course and coming about: *The sloop is on a reach, and the helmsman changes to a close-hauled course as the boom is hauled in. Before "coming about," or changing direction into the wind, the next maneuver, he makes sure the boat is sailing well and has good steerageway. The helmsman turns the boat into the wind and the jib begins to luff. The boom swings across as the boat coasts until it has turned 90 degrees and the wind is coming from the opposite side. The jib is set to fill on the new tack while the mainsail takes care of itself. Both sails fill, and the boat picks up speed on the new tack.*

▲ Now and then you may feel a little spray splashed into the air by the bow as it punches into the oncoming waves.

But things aren't always what they seem on the water. Sailing on a reach is the fastest point of sailing, sailing downwind *seems* slower than it really is, and sailing close-hauled *seems* the fastest but is often the slowest.

Just as you begin to think you have sailing in a straight line down pat, it's time to learn how to change direction. The next maneuver will be *coming about.*

Coming about. To come about, you will have to get the boat to turn quickly, directly into the wind, and then keep turning *through the wind* so that the wind comes from the other side; you'll still be sailing close-hauled, but it will be on the opposite *tack.*

Here are the major steps you'll take to come about:

▲ The person steering, the helmsman, pushes the tiller away from the windward side; this starts the boat turning into the wind.
▲ At the same time, the crew releases the

jibsheet that has been in use, the one opposite the windward side.

▲ The boom swings over by itself; the main sheet does not have be tended when coming about. On some boats, the boom rides high enough to clear the heads of people sitting in the boat, but in most small boats they need to duck. So learn this rule early: when coming about, *mind the boom.*

▲ As the boat heads off on her new course, the helmsman brings the tiller back to the center.

▲ At the same time, the helper hauls in on the other jibsheet, the one now on the opposite (leeward) side, which has just become the lower side of the boat. Both crew members have moved to sit on the high side.

When you tack—that is, when you come about, or sail close-hauled from one tack to the other—you end up making a turn that's approximately 90 degrees, as you can see in the diagrams on pages 36-37 and 39.

Look at the diagram on page 39 to see how a boat makes way in zigzag fashion against the wind. It's called *beating to windward* and it can be slow going, but it's the tacking that

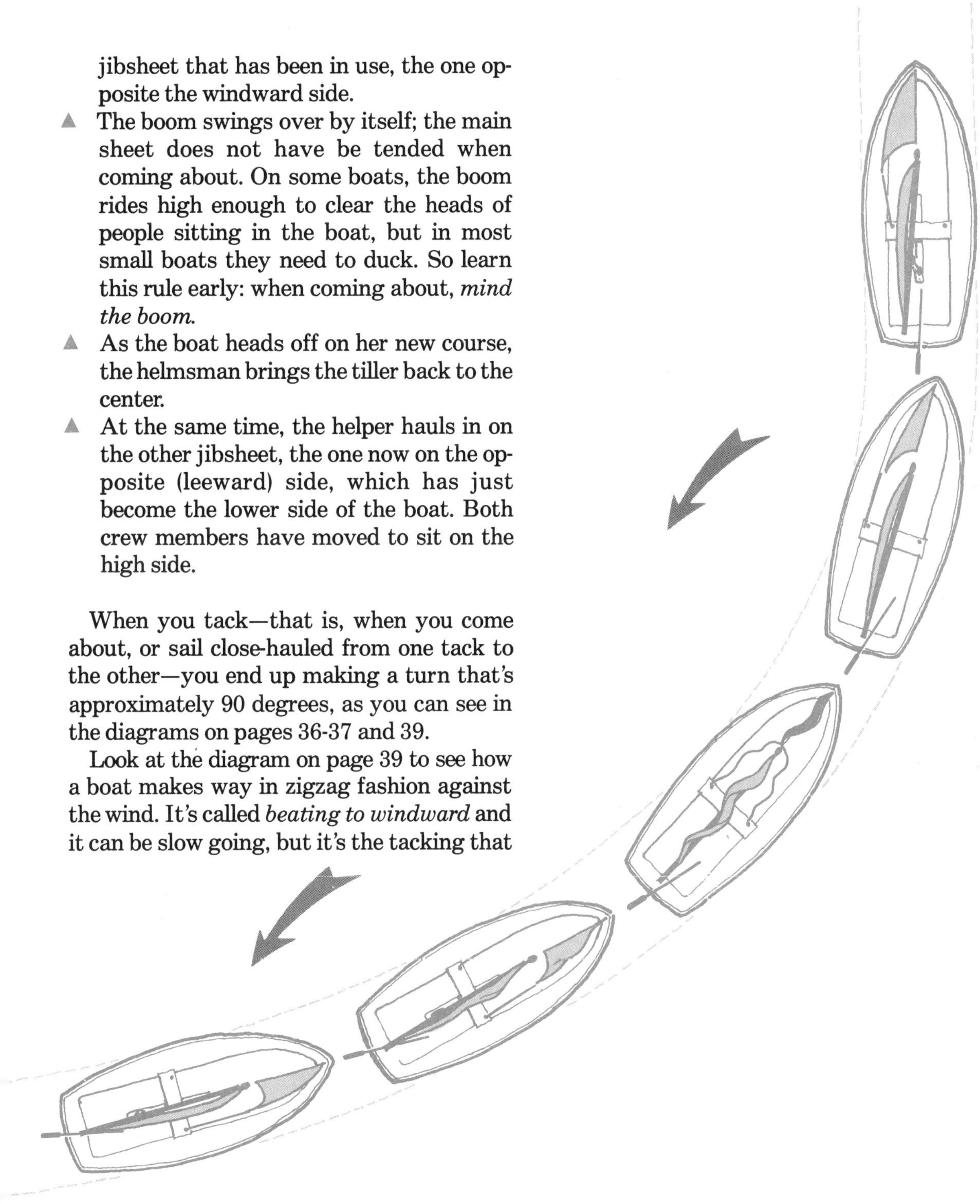

To come about may take as long as ten seconds, and the boat should be close-hauled when you begin (above, left). Push the tiller away from the direction in which you wish to go (above, right). The sails will luff as the boat turns into the wind. As the mainsail and jib swing over, release the jibsheet. Crew and skipper move to the other side (below, left). The mainsail takes care of itself and the opposite jibsheet is now adjusted (below, right).

gets you there. Later on, you'll learn there are various tricks to tacking, depending on the smoothness of the water on a particular day, the way the current is going, and exactly what sailing qualities a boat has, particularly how *close to the wind* she'll sail.

Luffing. Our little sloop is now moving smoothly on a new tack. Let's try to slow the boat and come as close as possible to stopping in the water with the sails still up. There will be times when you'll want to do this, perhaps to anchor, or to approach a dock, or simply to chat with someone in another boat.

Slowly head the boat into the wind until first the mainsail and then the jib begin to flutter. The fluttering is called *luffing* and so is the maneuver. For a minute or so the boat will keep coasting, just as if you were coming about. But, steering carefully, do not let the bow swing through the wind. Wait until the boat almost stops, then just in time, bring the tiller back up so that the sails fill and the boat starts sailing again on the same tack.

Jibing. One more maneuver to attempt now is going onto the other tack by turning the stern of the boat, instead, of the bow, through the wind. This is called *jibing,* and it's the opposite of tacking. Jibing is difficult: it *must* be done correctly, and it calls for everyone to move with smooth precision.

Here are the rudiments of the jibe. Again, before you jibe, you're sailing downwind, the

A series of tacks, alternately port and starboard, is the standard way to sail "against the wind." It's slow progress, even when the boat is fast. Note how the sails shift as the boat turns.

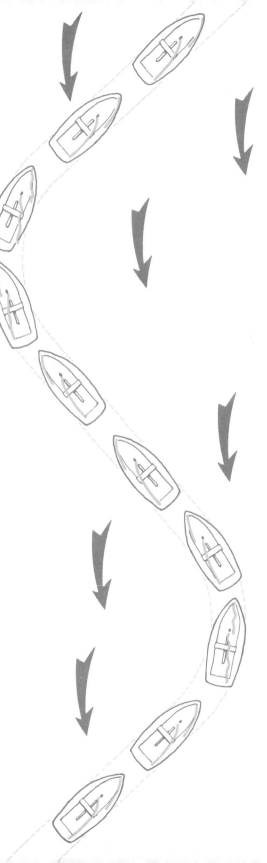

boom is well out, and the wind is coming partly from one side over the stern. As the decision to jibe is made, the crew member handling the mainsheet hauls it in until the boom is close to the centerline, or *amidships*. The helmsman keeps steering downwind, slowly turning the boat away from the wind (see the diagrams on pages 40 and 41). The jib comes over first, and you may sail wing and wing for a moment, then the mainsail swings quickly across to the other side of the boat. (Now you know why it was a good idea to haul that boom in close.) The crew moves, if necessary, to keep the weight distributed

---

Jibing: *Changing direction when the wind is behind the boat is called jibing. As the boat turns slowly, the mainsail is brought in. By the time the boom is amidships, the wind is directly astern. The boom, held close by the mainsheet, shifts over just as the jib begins to work on the new tack. Then the boom is let out.*

correctly. Once the jib starts pulling, the mainsheet is let out until the boom is again at right angles to the wind but on the opposite side from where it began. The helmsman continues to steer carefully to avoid turning into the wind. This is a potential problem in jibing that makes the boat difficult to control for a moment.

As you sail back to port, you can reflect that you've now tried all the points of sailing: close, beam, and broad reaching; off the wind, or running; and on the wind, or close-hauled. You've come about, you've tried luffing, and you've jibed. If that's all there were to sailing, you'd get your diploma after one lesson. But still to come are a great many practical matters: all the step-by-step procedures to start sailing, to leave and approach a dock, to take care of the sails, and to cope with dozens of variations in wind strength. Actually, you will never stop learning on a boat.

Some sailing theory. In case you're wondering just how a boat can sail *against the wind,* here's the explanation.

˙When the wind is abeam, it naturally pushes the boat sideways. That's why sailboats have movable centerboards or fixed keels—to resist the wind's sideways push with their lateral resistance against the water. If the boat can't move sideways, the wind's force against the sail tends to heel the boat over to some extent. A boat with a keel has a heavy weight in the keel to counteract this force, and a centerboarder's width and its crew's weight to windward do the same thing.

The trick is to convert that thwarted sideways force into a useful forward thrust. This is accomplished with a hull designed so its slips forward through the water easily and with sails shaped to act like vertical airplane wings, creating a lift that urges the boat forward.

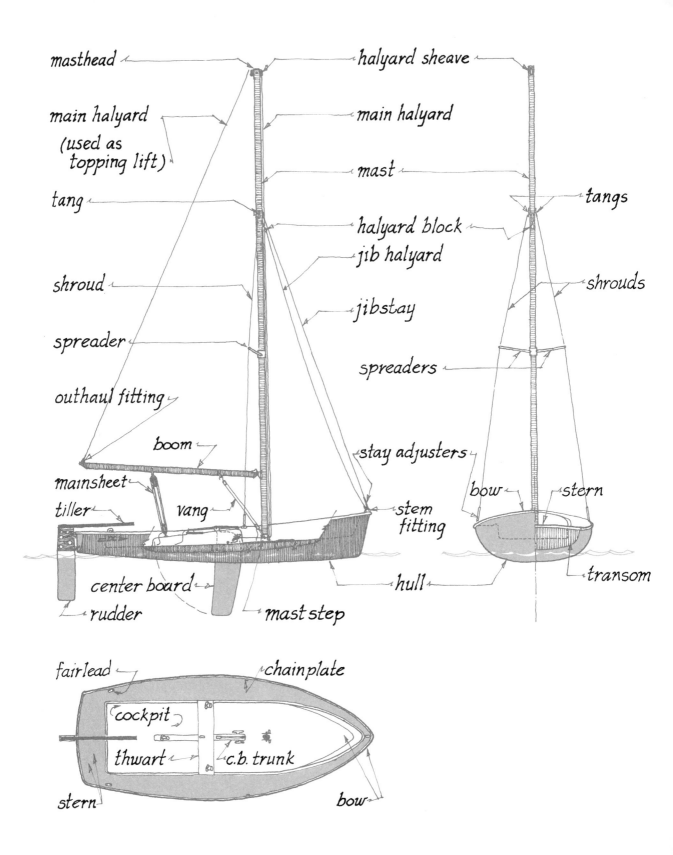

masthead

main halyard
(used as
topping lift)

tang

shroud

spreader

outhaul fitting

boom

mainsheet

tiller

vang

center board

rudder

mast step

halyard sheave

main halyard

mast

halyard block

jib halyard

jibstay

spreaders

stay adjusters

stem
fitting

hull

tangs

shrouds

bow

stern

transom

fairlead

chainplate

cockpit

thwart

c.b. trunk

stern

bow

3

ANATOMY OF A SLOOP

There may be more than a hundred nautical words that describe the anatomy of a sailboat, but fortunately, you probably already know a good many of them. In any case, we'll explain most of the common ones in this chapter. As you get to know the names of the parts of a sailboat, you'll realize that most of them have a specific and necessary function in helping a boat to sail.

Let's review the anatomy of Designer's Choice, the sloop shown in most of the accompanying illustrations. Like most boats

A close look at the parts of a typical sloop in the three drawings opposite will give you a better understanding of their names and functions.

today, the D-C is simple in design, with a minimum of extra gear. She has one mast and carries a jib and a mainsail. She is a centerboarder, with a housing, or *trunk,* in the middle, into which the *centerboard* is lifted when it's not being used to help sail the boat. The board pivots, and is raised and lowered by a line called the *centerboard pendant* (pronounced "pennant"). The centerboard helps to keep the boat from sliding sideways in the water.

The rudder is attached to the *transom* at the stern, and swings from side to side to steer the boat when you make a turn. It also functions to keep the boat sailing in a straight line, and helps prevent her from

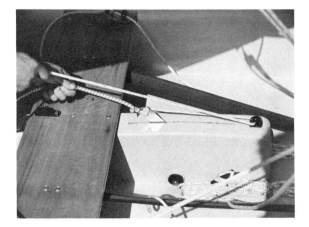

The centerboard is moved up or down on its pivot by adjusting the pendant (top line). Shock cord on the board eases the motion.

The rudder has a pivoting lower blade that swings up for beaching. A control line holds it in the desired position.

moving sideways, somewhat like an extra centerboard. On the D-C, the rudder blade pivots up and down, controlled from inside the boat with a line by which it can be raised when the boat is beached or hauled up on a trailer or float.

The *tiller* controls the rudder; on a DC the tiller has an extension that swings to either side, enabling you to sit on the high side of the boat, where your weight is needed, and still steer easily.

Other features of the D-C's hull are its built-in flotation and provision for self-bailing. This means that the boat can be easily righted after capsizing and that any water taken in soon drains out, as she starts sailing again. In Chapter 5, you'll learn the proper way to right a small sailboat after capsizing.

Spars and rigging. The mast and the boom are called *spars,* and all the wires and ropes attached to the spars and sails make up the *rigging.* The mast is secured in place at the bottom by the *mast step* (see pages 46, 57). The mast is held in place by the *standing rigging*—in the D-C it's the wire *jibstay* that runs to the bow and two other stays, *shrouds,* one each on the starboard and the port sides (see page 42). At their upper ends, the three stays are fastened to the mast with small fittings called *tangs.* The lower end of the jibstay is fastened to a fitting at the *stemhead*—the most forward part of the bow. The lower end of each shroud is fastened to the side of the hull with a stainless-steel fitting called a *chain plate.*

Since even stays and shrouds made of

The parts of triangular sails (the most common type) are identified in these drawings. Details show how the jib attaches to the jibstay with hanks, and how the mainsail is fastened to the mast with slides that fit into the mast slot.

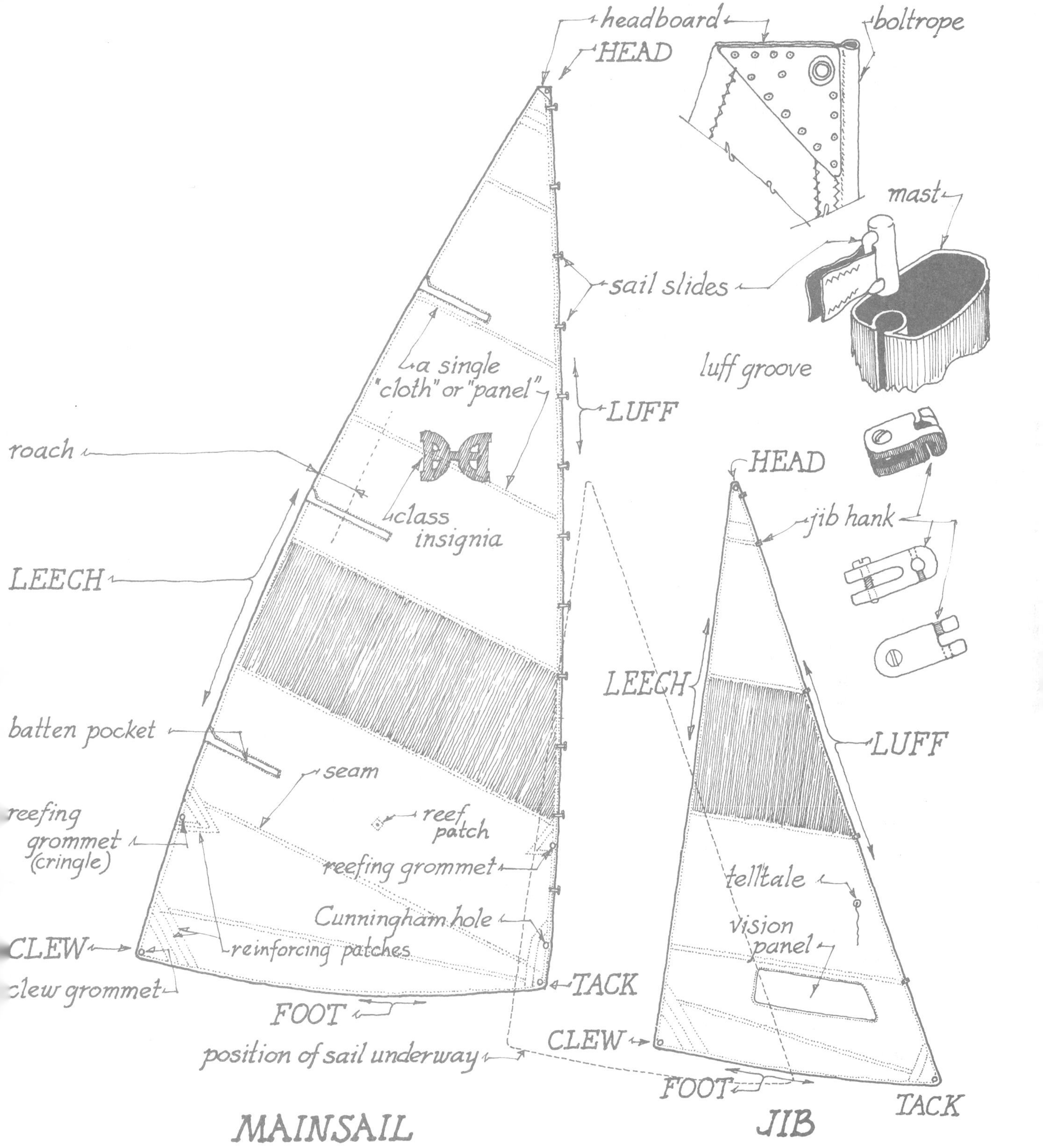

headboard

HEAD

boltrope

mast

sail slides

luff groove

LUFF

a single "cloth" or "panel"

roach

class insignia

LEECH

HEAD

jib hank

batten pocket

LEECH

seam

LUFF

reef patch

reefing grommet (cringle)

reefing grommet

telltale

Cunningham hole

vision panel

CLEW

reinforcing patches

clew grommet

TACK

FOOT

CLEW

position of sail underway

FOOT

TACK

MAINSAIL

JIB

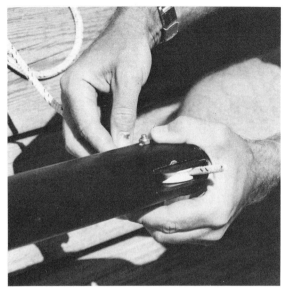

When rigging a D-C, put the halyard through the sheave at the masthead and attach the stays before stepping and raising the mast.

The mast, with stays and halyards in place, is brought aboard the boat; this sloop can be rigged on a trailer or after it has been launched.

stainless-steel wire stretch a little and need occasional adjusting, they are fitted at their lower ends with *turnbuckles,* rigging screws, or other ingenious adjusters.

The *running rigging* (as opposed to the standing rigging), usually made of braided Dacron rope, is used primarily to control the sails or anything else that moves, such as the centerboard pendant. The jib *halyard* raises the *jib.* On a D-C, it goes through a *block* high on the mast, runs down the mast, and is securely cleated. (Ashore, you would call a block a pulley.)

Similarly, the main halyard is used to hoist the *mainsail.* The main halyard also goes up the mast, around a built-in masthead block called a *sheave* (pronounced "shiv"), and down the forward side of the mast. Both the

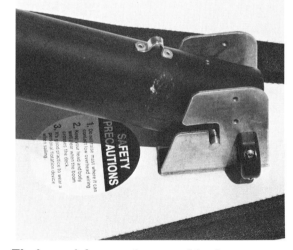

The base of the mast is secured in the mast step (above), and the shrouds are fastened to the chain plates before the mast is raised.

An aluminum mast is easily raised by two people. If the boat were on a trailer, the helper could pull on the jib halyard from the ground.

One person steadies the mast while the other fastens the jibstay turnbuckle to the bow fitting. Next, the shrouds are made fast.

A stainless-steel ring secures the jibstay turnbuckle to the fitting. The turnbuckle is tightened by turning the knob at the top.

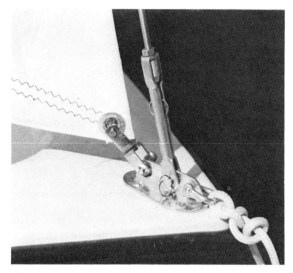

The tack of the jib is fastened to the fitting, behind the turnbuckle, and the mooring line is attached to the shackle (forward).

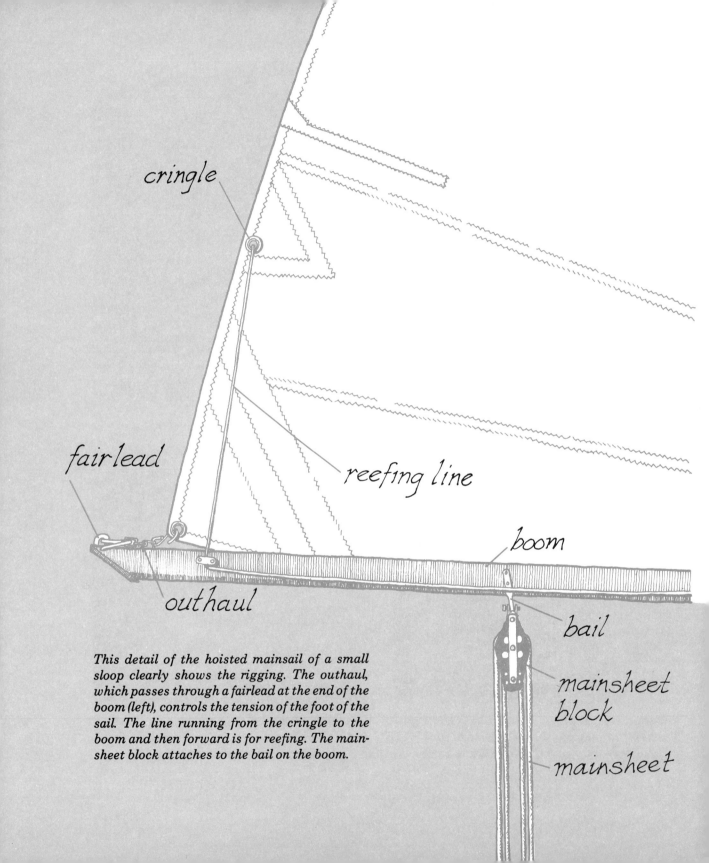

cringle

fairlead

reefing line

boom

outhaul

bail

mainsheet
block

mainsheet

This detail of the hoisted mainsail of a small sloop clearly shows the rigging. The outhaul, which passes through a fairlead at the end of the boom (left), controls the tension of the foot of the sail. The line running from the cringle to the boom and then forward is for reefing. The mainsheet block attaches to the bail on the boom.

jib and main halyards lead to *cleats* on the side of the centerboard trunk, to which they are fastened after the sails have been hoisted.

When sailing, you need to be able to control the jib: let it out or pull it in a bit, depending on how you're sailing. This is done with two lines, or *jibsheets*, which are fastened to the lower rear corner, or *clew*, of the jib. One sheet goes to each side of the boat, where they are fed through smooth, round fittings called *fairleads*, which prevent chafing, and then to cleats. On the D-C the fairlead has a built-in cam cleat. However, only one sheet is used, or cleated down, at a time. The sheet that's working has tension on it; the other one should be completely slack.

The mainsail is controlled by the *mainsheet*, which is rigged to the boom through a set of double blocks that make hauling in the sail easier, especially in a strong wind. The mainsheet can be cleated when you have it where you want it, but on small boats you generally hold it in your hand.

Another way to become familiar with rigging details on modern boats of various sizes is to look at a catalogue published by a rigging and marine-hardware manufacturer. Nicro-Fico, Schaeffer, Merriman-Holbrook, and others have especially informative catalogues. And if you get a chance to visit a sailmaker's loft someday, take advantage of the opportunity to see how sails are made. Pick a time when rush jobs are not the priorty. Usually fall or winter are best, except in the south.

The boom attaches to the mast with a gooseneck fitting, and is locked in place by a cotter pin (hanging on line). The center vang, also on a bail, helps keep the boom down. A line in the lower cringle, called the Cunningham, is used to adjust the draft in the sail. The upper cringle is used for the forward reef line.

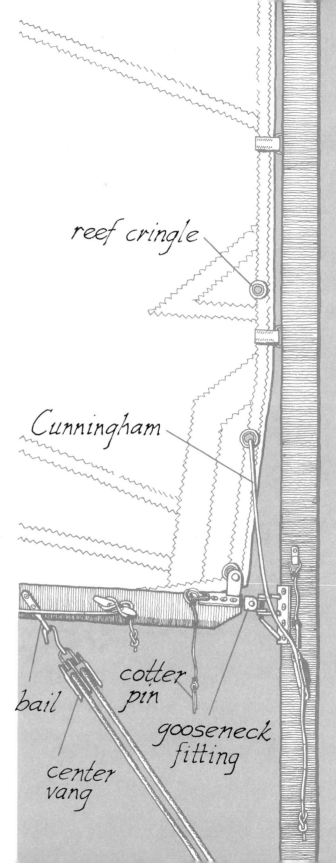

reef cringle

Cunningham

bail

cotter pin

gooseneck fitting

center vang

Sails. Now let's turn our attention to the sails. With very few exceptions, modern sails are basically triangular. The forward edge of a sail is called the *luff*. The mainsail on the D-C has special slides fastened to the luff, which fit into and are hoisted up in a special groove in the mast. The system is an ingenious one, made possible by modern inventions such as extruded aluminum masts and Delrin, a very strong plastic. The old-fashioned mast hoops, made of hickory or ash, that were used to encircle the masts on old boats were picturesque but not as efficient. Other modern boats may have other arrangements of bronze or plastic slides and stainless-steel track to hold the luff of the sail close to the mast.

The side of the sail opposite the luff is called the *leech*, and the lower side is called the *foot*. Another term to get straight is *roach*, meaning the outward-curving area along the leech of most sails that gives them a little extra area to trap the wind. On the mainsail the roach is prevented from curling over by *battens*, small stiffeners set into pockets sewn in the sail (see page 45).

The three corners of a triangular sail are the *head*, or top; the *tack*, or forward lower corner; and the *clew*, the lower rear, or after, corner. Each corner is reinforced, and fitted with a metal grommet or ring, making a hole called a *cringle*, by which the corner can be secured. On larger boats cringles have hand-sewn reinforcements, which are handsome examples of the sailmaker's art. The head, to which the halyard for hoisting the sail is attached, takes considerable strain and is therefore reinforced; the whole assemblage is called the *headboard*.

Each jibsheet, port and starboard, goes through a fairlead (right) to a cam cleat with teeth. Lifting the end of the sheet on the left instantly releases it from the cleat.

The mainsail. On the D-C, the mainsail is *loose-footed*, that is, it is attached to the boom only at the tack and clew. The clew fitting, on the outer end of the boom, is adjustable by means of the boom *outhaul* (see drawing, page 48). This line must be pulled taut and made fast so that the foot of the sail has no wrinkles.

On many boats the foot of the mainsail is attached to the boom continuously from tack to clew with slides set into a track or groove, like the luff. The reasons for the variations in these details have to do with the size of the sail and the intended use of the boat. The D-C's particular details are quite appropriate for day sailing and racing. When the wind is strong, you can tighten the outhaul on the boom (see page 55) to flatten the mainsail. If

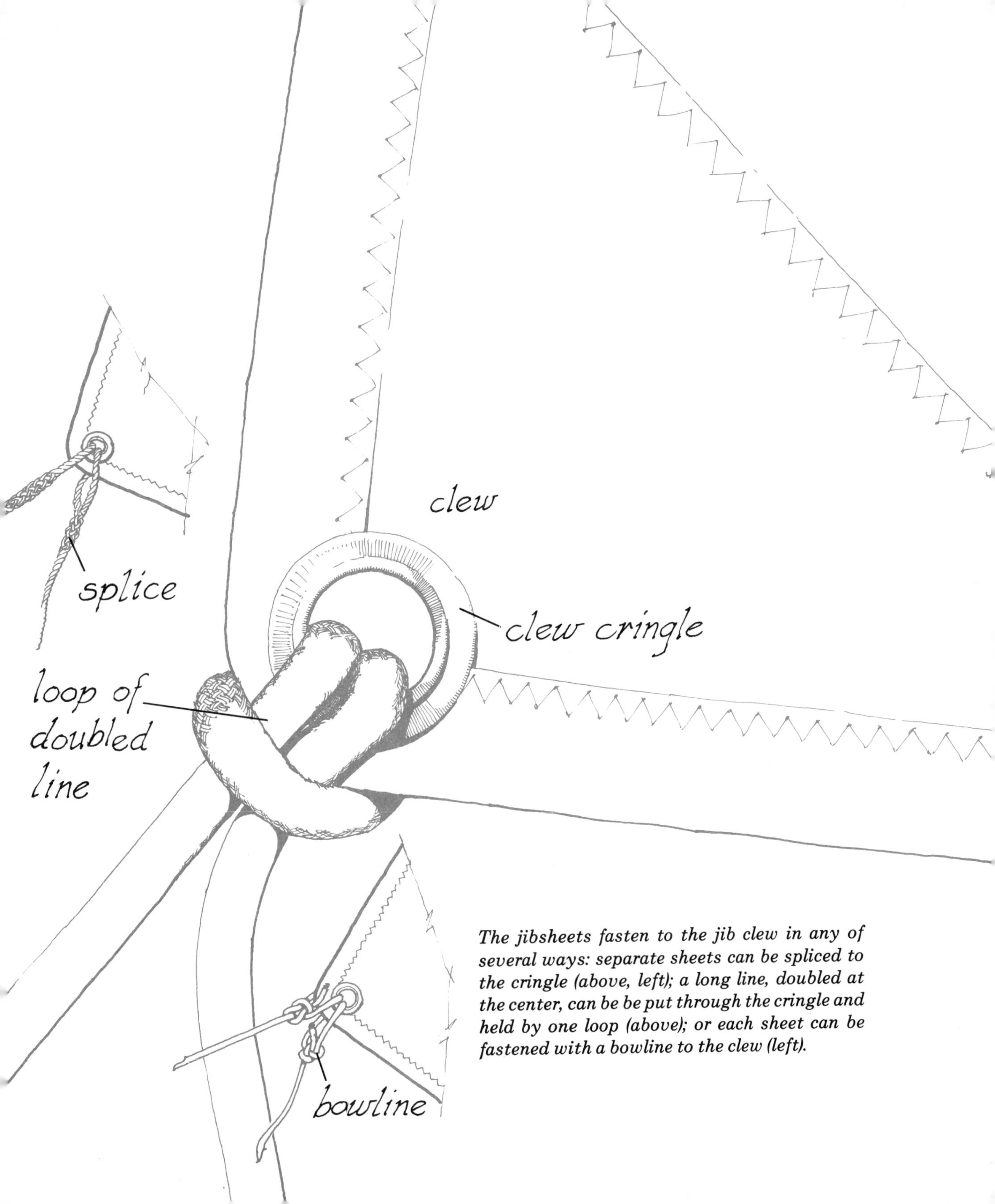

splice

clew

clew cringle

loop of
doubled
line

bowline

The jibsheets fasten to the jib clew in any of
several ways: separate sheets can be spliced to
the cringle (above, left); a long line, doubled at
the center, can be be put through the cringle and
held by one loop (above); or each sheet can be
fastened with a bowline to the clew (left).

TEN VITAL RIGGING PARTS

The rigging fittings shown here are found on a typical small sloop: the block, called a pulley on land, changes the direction of a line such as the jib halyard; the mainsheet block and cam cleat are precise controls for the mainsheet; fairleads change the angles of lines with minimum friction; cleats are used to hold halyards that are hauled taut; the jib fairlead with its cam cleat is shown in use on page 50; the jam cleat is used for the centerboard pendant; vernier adjusters adjust the tension of shrouds; turnbuckles are used for standing rigging; the halyard shackle has a loss-proof pin; and the jibstay is adjusted at the stemhead fitting with a stainless-steel turnbuckle. Most modern sailboats have rigging fittings similar to those shown here.

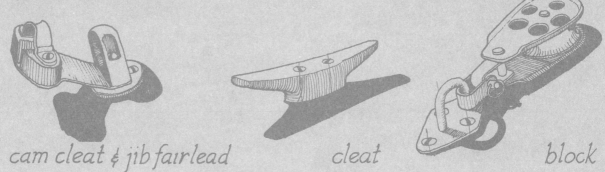

mainsheet block & cam cleat

cam cleat & jib fairlead   cleat   block

the wind turns light, you can ease the outhaul, to get the extra curve in the sail.

The jib. The tack of the jib is attached to the stemhead fitting with a *shackle.* As on a larger boat, this shackle pivots so that the sail will set smoothly.

Delrin slides hold the luff of the jib to the jibstay. The jib halyard is made fast to the head of the jib in the same way that the main halyard is attached to the mainsail.

You may notice that the sails aren't flat.

The mainsail, especially, has a very nice set of curves to it, put in by the sailmaker to give it an efficient aerodynamic shape when the sail is properly set up. When you're sailing close-hauled, most of the curve is close to the luff in the forward third of the sail, and the sail flattens out along the battens. Aircraft wings have the same basic shape, and so do the wings of a soaring bird.

Other details. Up to this point we've named the basic parts of the boat, the rigging, and

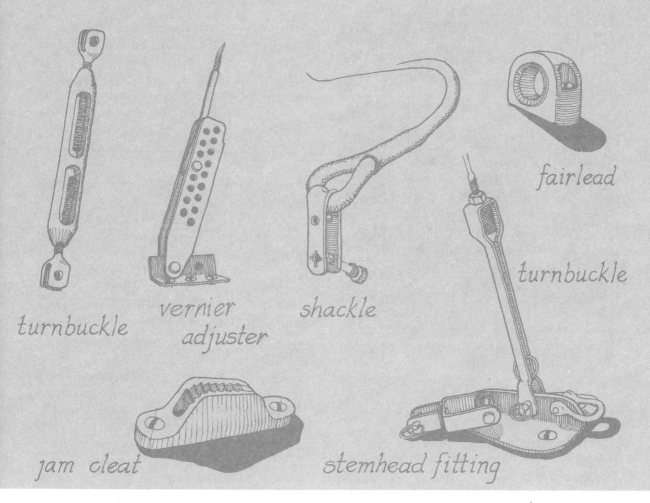

turnbuckle

vernier
adjuster

shackle

fairlead

turnbuckle

jam cleat

stemhead fitting

the sails, and we've described their functions. In later chapters, you'll learn more about how these various parts are handled when the boat is under way. But now let's take another look around so you can see some additional details on the boat.

First, let's look a little more closely at some of the running rigging and how it works, because skillful handling of the running rigging gives you the precise control of the boat that is the secret of sailing.

The jibsheets can be fastened to the clew of the jib in several ways. The drawing on page 51 shows a good method, if you have one long line that serves as both sheets. Another satisfactory arrangement consists of two separate sheets, each tied to the clew with a *bowline,* an extremely useful knot that neither slips nor jams (see page 135). Or the sheets can be spliced to the clew cringle. On larger boats, where the sheets might have to be changed on a long passage or during a race, they are sometimes attached with shackles. But shackles clatter when they hit

The boom attaches to the mast with a pin-type gooseneck and is held in place with a cotter pin (not visible). The hanging cotter pin holds the sail slides in the mast groove.

the mast and hurt when they hit your ears, so, for most purposes, bowlines are better.

The D-C also has an ingenious rigging device called a *center boom vang,* which is like the mainsheet except that it is seldom adjusted. It serves to control the shape of the mainsail by holding the boom down even when the boom is far out on a downwind course. This keeps the sail aerodynamically efficient. It does not, however, prevent an accidental jibe.

One innovation made possible by the use of new kinds of materials is a clear plastic window in the jib that makes it easier to keep a lookout ahead and to leeward. (Leeward, pronounced "loo'ard," is the opposite of windward, pronounced "wind'ard".)

In the photographs you will observe one other nicety of the D-C: toe straps, which are a convenience for racing. If you're *hiking,* or sitting way out on the high side, it's handy to hook your toes into these straps. You'll find them only on small boats, where it's necessary to get your weight out to windward to keep the boat from heeling too much.

Other common rigging. Two standard rigging items not found on a boat rigged as simply as the D-C, but seen on some similar-size boats and all larger ones are a *topping lift* and a *backstay.* A topping lift is a line or wire leading from the end of the boom to the masthead to hold the boom up when the sail is not hoisted. The D-C's boom is light enough to be held by hand during brief moments when the sail itself is not holding the boom up.

A backstay is a piece of standing rigging used on bigger boats to help support the mast. It is made of wire and runs from the masthead to the stern of the boat.

Larger boats frequently carry several jibs and other light sails, so that you have a choice of sails to set in varying wind conditions. If you happen to be getting your first sailing lessons aboard a larger, more elaborate boat than a D-C, you can identify most of these alternate sails and lines by referring to Chapter 6, "Other Boats, Other Rigs."

SETTING UP A D-C

With a small, trailerable boat such as the D-C, you may have to set up the rigging—that is, put the mast and boom in place and set up the standing rigging—each time you sail the boat. It's a ten-minute task, and the basic steps are shown in the photographs.

FASTENING AND SECURING THE OUTHAUL

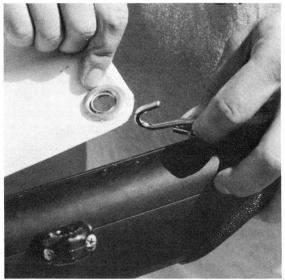

The outhaul is fastened to the mainsail clew with a simple hook that is slipped onto the cringle. Larger boats have bulkier fittings.

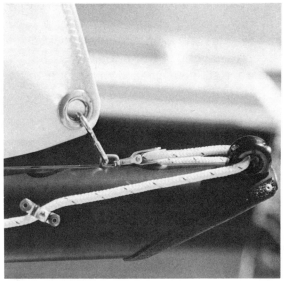

The outhaul (line) leads through a fairlead at the end of the boom (right), then forward along the boom, where it is secured.

The outhaul is fastened securely to a cleat on the boom with figure-eight turns; there must be proper tension on the outhaul.

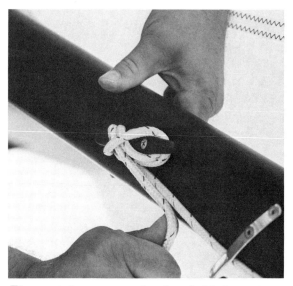

Figure-eight turns on the cleat hold the outhaul securely. See Chapter 9 for information on proper way to cleat a line.

When the boat is rigged, you must make a rapid but thorough inspection of every item before you start sailing. As you gain experience, this sort of constant inspection becomes second nature whenever you go aboard—but you have to make it a habit.

Always ask yourself: Are the pins holding the shrouds and jibstay securely in place (and if the cotter pins are not the circular kind—see page 47—are they taped to prevent tears, gashes, and other nuisances)?

Are the sheets and halyards properly led,

The D-C illustrated here is rigged, with the jib halyard ready for hoisting. The main halyard is not attached to the headboard, since it is being used as a temporary boom, or topping, lift.

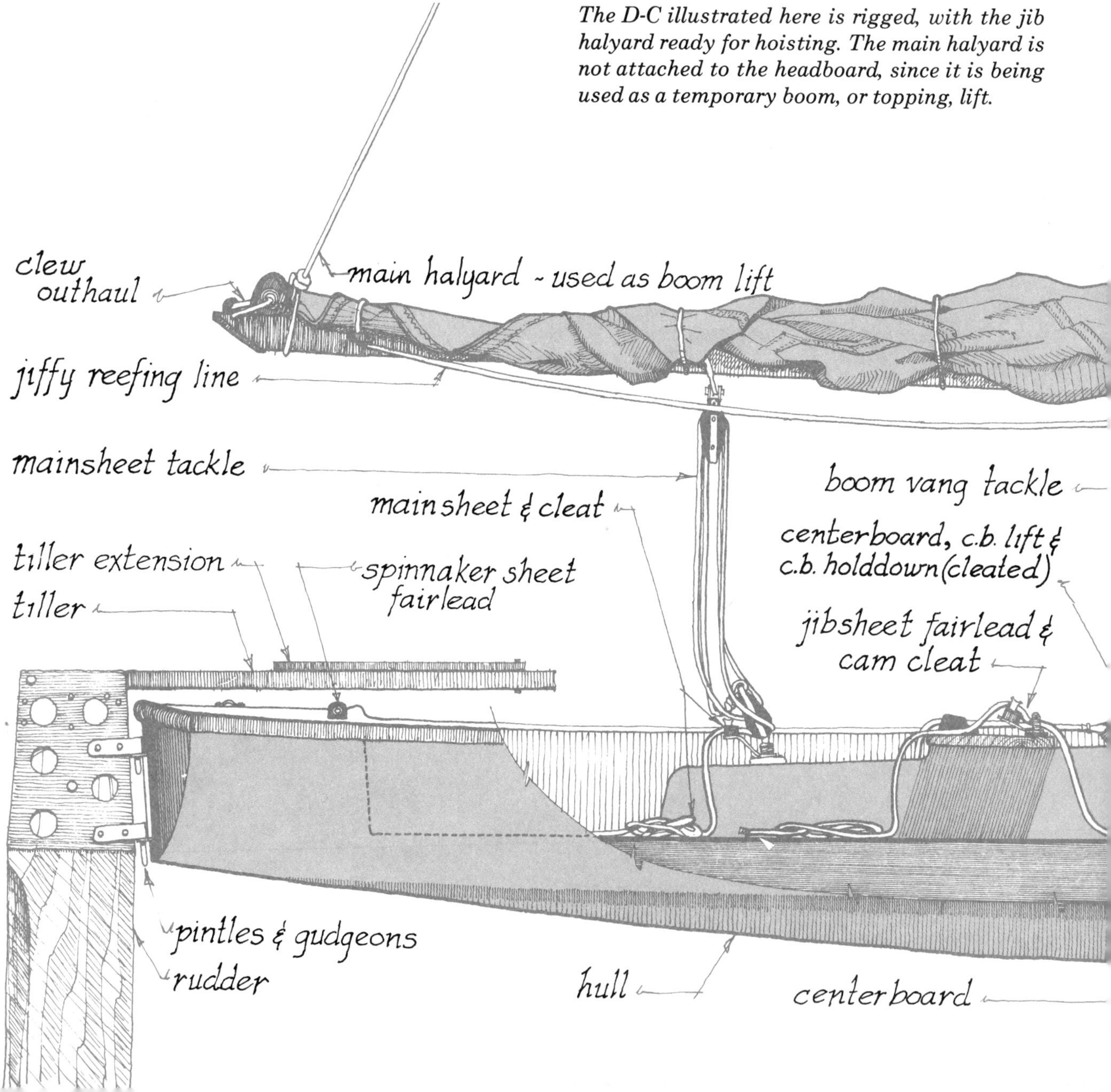

clew outhaul

main halyard - used as boom lift

jiffy reefing line

mainsheet tackle

mainsheet & cleat

boom vang tackle

centerboard, c.b. lift & c.b. holddown (cleated)

tiller extension

spinnaker sheet fairlead

jibsheet fairlead & cam cleat

tiller

pintles & gudgeons

rudder

hull

centerboard

and not in a tangle? Are the battens in place, or aboard the boat ready to be inserted? Are the rudder and centerboard properly fitted and checked out?

The final drawing shows the D-C, rigged, with sails attached, or *bent on*. The boom, with mainsail furled, appears to be held up as if by an invisible hand, but it's really supported by the main halyard acting as a temporary topping lift.

Now that everything has been checked, you're ready to go sailing, one step at a time.

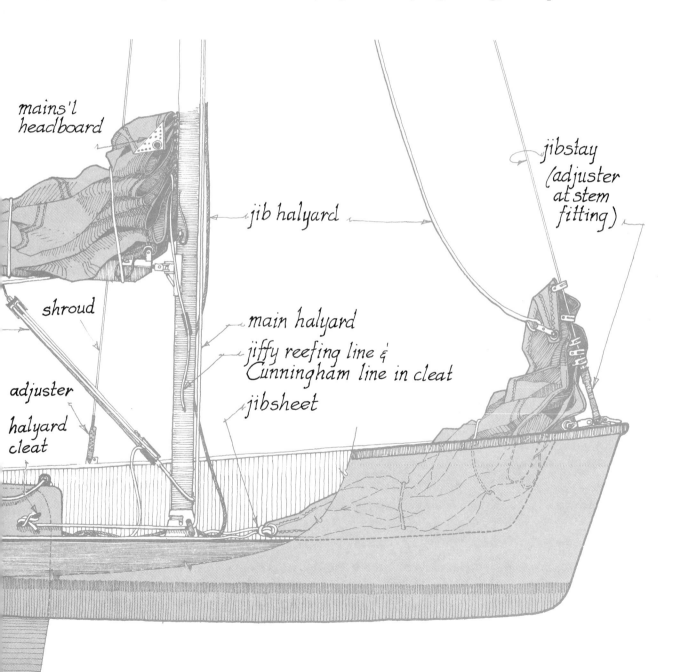

mains'l headboard

jib halyard

jibstay
(adjuster at stem fitting)

shroud

main halyard

jiffy reefing line &
Cunningham line in cleat

jibsheet

adjuster

halyard cleat

FOUR STEPS IN STARTING OUT

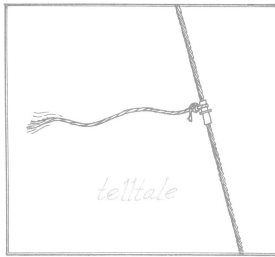

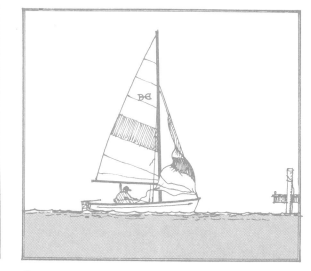

1. *Before raising the mainsail, check the wind direction by glancing at the telltale on the shroud. Be sure the boat heads into the wind.*

2. *Next, check to make sure there are no tangles in the sheets or halyards and that all rigging and equipment are in place.*

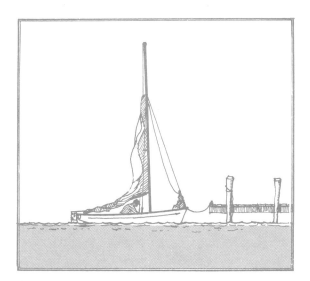

3. *Haul up the mainsail and cleat the halyard taut; then raise the jib until the halyard is very taut, and cleat it down.*

4. *Adjust the mainsheet and trim the jibsheet to set the sails properly for the point of sailing you intend; here the boat is on a reach.*

4

SAILING STEP BY STEP

Now you're going sailing on your own. You've had your basic instruction and a practice sail; this time, instead of an instructor, take a competent crew member with you and start putting what you've learned into practice.

PLANNING THE DAY'S SAIL

Before starting out on a day's sail you will need to plan your steps ahead, and your first thought should be for the wind. Which way is it blowing? The answer will determine the direction you take when you start. How hard is it blowing? Is there a forecast for changing wind? How are the boats that are already out on the water doing? Are they drifting in a

near calm, or heeling over and sailing fast?

If you are in a salt-water area, is the tide going to be a factor—either because of the depth of the water or because of the tide running in or out of the harbor? All these bits of information are quickly absorbed once you get into the habit of looking. Although at first you will need to make conscious plans to fit each situation, you will eventually learn to make decisions almost subconsciously.

Your second look will be to the boat. She should be properly rigged, with the sails and safety equipment on board, and tied to the dock almost ready to go. You make a quick check to see that the boom is securely attached to the mast at the gooseneck fitting,

When you get ready to hoist the sails, first fasten the jib hanks to the jibstay, and then put the halyard shackle pin through the headboard.

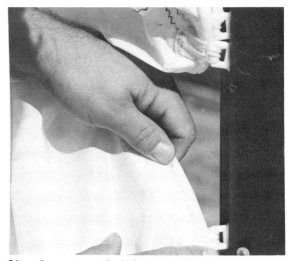

Slip the mainsail slides into the groove in the mast, making sure the slides are not twisted. A pin holds the bottom slide in place.

and that the rudder has been properly installed. Check that the centerboard is down and all the standing rigging is properly set up (this means that the jibstay is taut and that both shrouds are reasonably taut). As for the running rigging, make sure the center boom vang is in place and the mainsheet is properly rigged at the outer end of the boom.

Preparing to hoist the sails. Normally you will hoist the mainsail first and the jib second, but if your crew is helping, you can get both sails ready at the same time. The boat should be heading into the wind.

The preliminary steps for the mainsail are these: the tack and clew are hooked on, as shown in the preceding chapter. The outhaul is adjusted so that the foot of the sail is almost tight. The battens are inserted in the pockets. (On some sails the battens may vary

in length; usually the shorter ones go top and bottom.) You fasten the halyard shackle, with its nonremovable pin that twists shut, to the headboard, after you take a look aloft to make sure the halyard is not wrapped around anything. And you insert the sail slides in the mast slot, starting with the slide nearest the head of the sail.

Hoisting the sails. Now for the normal sequence of getting the sails up. The main goes up first. As on most boats, the main halyard on our D-C is on the starboard side. If you've checked the boat, the wind, and nearby boats that might be in your way, it's time to sail.

Let's say the wind is moderate, so there will be no problems getting under way. Haul the main halyard tight—very tight—and cleat it down (see Chapter 9 for the right way to cleat a line). Take a quick look at the mainsheet to

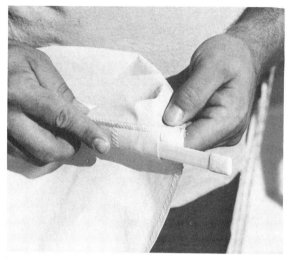

Insert the battens into the pockets on the mainsail before hoisting. Battens keep the roach of the sail flat.

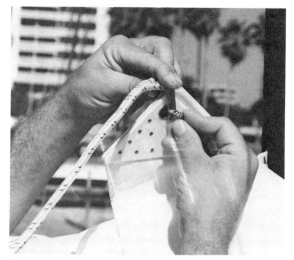

Fasten the mainsail halyard shackle to the headboard, and make sure that the halyard is running free and is not caught on the spreaders.

make sure everything is still clear. The wind should be blowing from straight ahead and the boom slatting idly back and forth. If you tighten the sheet, the slatting will stop—but don't do it until you're ready to go, because the moment the sail fills, the boat will start moving.

Hoisting the jib. The halyard (on the port side of the mast) needs only a few rapid hand-over-hand hauls, and the jib is up. Give the halyard an extra pull, with your legs braced, and then cleat it down. Now you're ready to sail. Get the crew aboard and cast off the dock lines. Give a push to get the bow off the dock, so that you're heading in the right direction, and have your hand on the tiller so you can start steering as soon as the sails fill and the boat begins to move.

As you start sailing, adjust the mainsheet

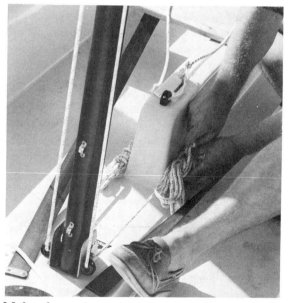

Make the main and jib halyards fast to their cleats after you have hauled up the sails. Coil the end of the line to keep it out of the way.

and then the jibsheet, so that both sails are working efficiently as you steer your intended course.

Here we should say a word about sheets on small boats. In moderate winds, the jibsheet on the D-C will probably be cleated, using the *cam cleat,* once the sail is set correctly. The cam cleat, which has spring-loaded jaws that grip the line between them, allows the sheet to release instantly when the line is pulled up sharply out of the jaws. The mainsheet, in good small-boat sailing practice, is kept in the helmsman's hand, which makes small adjustments easy. It is also a safety precaution: if there's a strong puff of wind when you're reaching or sailing close-hauled, the mainsheet can be eased quickly to prevent excessive heeling. If the wind is steady and you want to open your lunch with your free hand, you may cleat the mainsheet too—for a short time. On a large cruising boat, *all* the sheets are cleated, but in such a way that they can be cast off in a hurry.

Out on the water at last, but this time you're not the passive observer you were in Chapter 2, trying to get the feeling and

Coming about, step by step: *The helmsman holds the tiller steady, makes sure the boat is sailing well, and then says "Ready about!" In response, the crew checks the jibsheets, removes any tangles, and gets set to cast off the working sheet at the proper moment (1). The helmsman calls "Hard alee!" and moves the tiller to start the turn; the boat swings into the wind. As the jib and main luff, both helmsman and crew move to the other side of the boat (2).*

1

2

picture of sailing. Now you're doing the sailing yourself.

Coming about. You have already learned the basics of coming about, but let's go over in detail the sequence of steps for coming about when you're close-hauled:

▲ Look around to make sure no other boat or obstruction will be in the way after you tack. Remember that you'll be making a right-angle turn, so you should look pretty much off the beam to windward.

▲ Make sure the boat is sailing well. She needs to have good speed through the water, and she should be sailing as close to the wind as she'll go.

▲ Say "Ready about!" This warns your crew that you're about to tack and that he or she should look to the jibsheets. The one in use, the leeward sheet, is quickly checked to make sure the loose end is free to run with no snarls. The jibsheet that will be used *after* you come about, the one now on the windward side, is similarly checked so that it's ready to hand.

As the bow swings to the other side, the boom automatically swings over and the crew casts off the working jibsheet and picks up the opposite jibsheet, ready to pull it in (3). As the helmsman straightens the tiller and the main begins to fill, the crew hauls in the jibsheet and adjusts it so the sail is working efficiently. The boat, having coasted through the eye of the wind, now picks up speed (4).

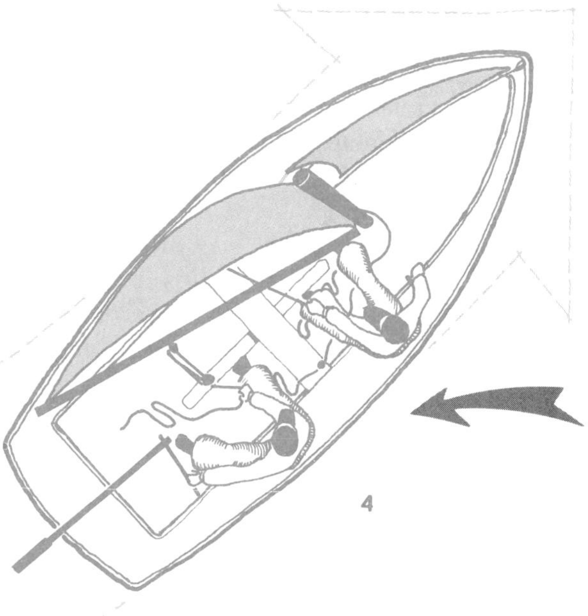

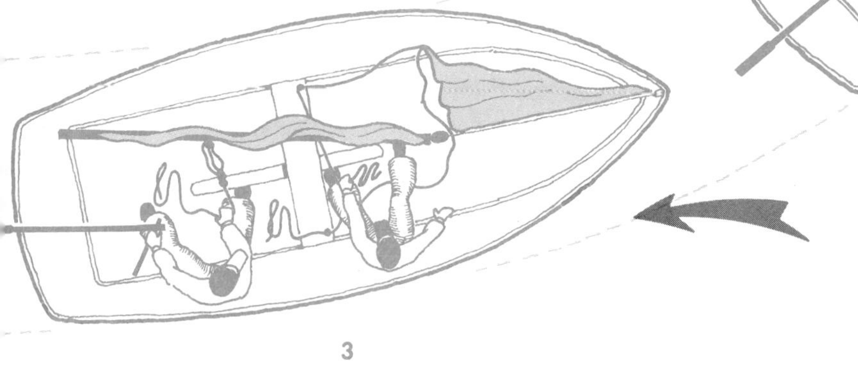

- Say "Hard alee!" and push the tiller down, toward the boom. Not too fast, not too far. You want to turn the boat, not yank it around.
- As the boat turns into the wind, the jib begins to luff. When the jib is no longer working at all—when it's even with the mast—your crew smartly casts off the cleated sheet and moves across to take in the other sheet.
- By now the boom is amidships, and as the boat turns through the wind, the boom swings across. Always be prepared to duck. The boom doesn't have far to travel, so you don't have to do anything about adjusting the mainsheet. But you do have to move to the new high side of the boat as she swings.
- At just about the same time as the boom is amidships, your crew brings in the new jibsheet, *but not until the boat is all the way through the wind.* He or she gradually pulls in the sheet until it is adjusted correctly and then slips it into the cam cleat—on the low, or leeward, side of the boat. As the boat heels, the crew moves up to sit on the high side with you.

You've come about.

Note: if you had been sailing on a reach and wanted to come about, you would first come up nearer the wind, trim your sails, and then proceed as just described.

Getting in irons and out. Can something go wrong when you're coming about? Yes, if the boat doesn't keep moving or if you have forgotten to make allowance for any special condition, the boat can stall.

Suppose you are sailing with a light breeze in choppy water, without enough headway. As you head the boat into the wind, she slows up, and, instead of coasting through the wind to the opposite tack, she gets hung up—stalled. It's called *getting in irons* or, sometimes, *in stays.* It can happen if your crew takes up on the new jibsheet too soon so that the wind gets on the wrong side of the jib and stops the turn. Here are the ways to deal with the problem of tacking in light air.

If you foresee the situation and know the conditions are adverse, your crew should be ready. All that's usually needed is to back the jib at just the right moment. This means the jib is held out by hand, still on the original side until the wind catches it on the back side. If you're still coasting a bit, the wind in the jib will push the bow over.

This is the easiest solution, but it won't work if you lose all forward motion. In that case your rudder is useless, because it works only when the boat is moving through the water. Now you really are in irons—but don't get flustered. Pretty soon the boat will begin to move backward, pushed by the wind, and then the rudder will begin to work again—but in *the opposite way.* Often you can put the tiller to the other side to get the boat turned—either onto the new tack or back on the old one so you can try again. Once the boat is at the correct angle to the wind, the sails will start working again so you can reverse the tiller and start sailing forward.

Another solution is to cast off the mainsheet and push the boom out horizontally to leeward. Now you'll truly start sailing backward and can use the rudder the opposite way to get the boat pointed right.

It's a good idea to put yourself in irons purposely a few times just to practice getting

When the D-C is sailing—on a fast reach, for example—the tiller extension enables the *helmsman to sit on the high side. Both the main- and jibsheets are held by hand.*

out. Once you have tried all the solutions and have the feel of the boat, you may go for weeks without getting in irons. It should be added that it isn't only in light winds that this happens. Misjudge your speed and timing under almost any conditions and you can get in irons.

Jibing. A controlled, intentional jibe is a necessary, standard maneuver, easily learned. When sailing downwind, you use it to alter course in the direction away from the side the wind is on. Remember that when tacking you put the bow through the wind; when jibing, you put the stern through.

The following steps constitute the procedure for a proper jibe:

▲ Alert your crew, usually by saying, "It's time to jibe."
▲ The crew looks to the jibsheets, which are easy to handle; sometimes they're slack.

▲ Continuing to steer on the same course, you take up on the mainsheet until the boom is as close to midships as possible. The wind is still blowing from behind you, and the mainsail won't be doing much for the moment. Now say, loudly, "Jibe-O."

▲ Slowly you alter course (see diagram, page 67). Normally this is not a big change, just enough to get the wind on the other side of the mainsail. Now the boom swings over, just a short distance, because the sheet is controlling it.

▲ At about the same time, your crew lets go of one jibsheet, and takes up on the opposite one.

▲ Quickly but smoothly and keeping control of things, you let out the mainsheet until the boom is out again on the other side. If you're sailing downwind, this means the boom is again at right angles to the wind. If you want to keep coming around to sail on a reach on the new tack, you turn farther, but let the boom out only partway.

Proper sail trim. Now, let's work on the proper trim of the sails.

For each kind of sailing—close-hauled, close reaching, broad reaching, and sailing downwind—there's an optimum trim of the sails. You want both sails to be working to maximum effect. Here's how it's done. Start with the main, letting it out until the forward edge of the sail starts to luff, then pull it back in just enough to stop the luff. Now do the

---

The accidental jibe: *An accidental jibe, always dangerous, occurs when the boom swings over unexpectedly (from port to starboard in this case). Injury to crew or boat can result.*

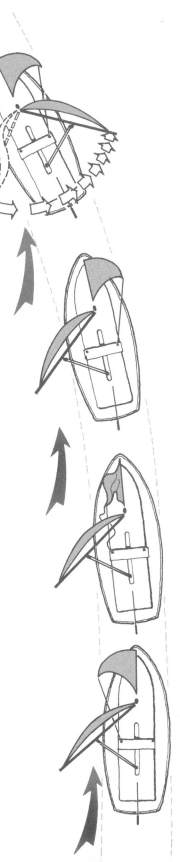

same with the jib. You may have to trim the main again, since the jib affects the main by sending a draft of air past its luff.

Telltales. One way to keep track of where the wind's blowing is to use *telltales*. These are simple but extremely useful devices that indicate the direction of the wind, and you should never sail without them. To make a telltale, tie a small length of knitting yarn or a strip of nylon stocking to each shroud. The strips should be high enough to catch the wind, but not so high that you get a crick in your neck from watching them. You can also buy little red feathers or plastic telltales. And there are a couple of special telltales built into the luffs of some jibs (including the D-C's) that indicate the airflow over the jib. When the jib is trimmed right, its telltales should be streaming straight back.

Learn to watch the telltales. Get the feel of fast sailing, on the wind or reaching, and note how your telltales fly. Then you'll be able to duplicate the angle next time. When the wind is astern, the telltale may be less helpful, but you can switch to another sensitive instrument: the back of your neck.

Downwind sailing. Sensitivity to the wind's direction is important at all times, but never

---

The controlled jibe: *To make a controlled jibe, be sure the wind is coming from directly astern (1). Then bring the boom to the center of the boat with the mainsheet and turn the rudder gradually as the wind catches the jib and swings it over gently (2). The jib fills and the mainsail swings over sharply (3). As soon as the boom shifts, let the mainsheet out smoothly (4). No swoosh, just a steady change of direction.*

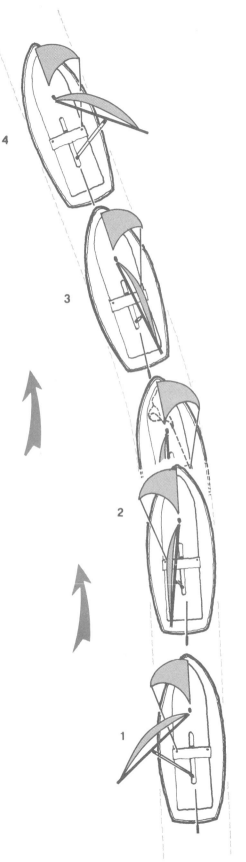

THE QUICK JIBE

Experienced sailors start a quick jibe—a safe procedure only in light airs—by hauling in the mainsheet quickly as the turn is started.

Both helmsman and crew duck and change sides as the boom swings over under full control, and the jibsheet on the other side is hauled in.

The helmsman keeps the boat turning smoothly and lets the mainsheet out slowly as the wind catches the sail from the other side.

The boat settles on the new course, with the boom set well out and the jib drawing fully. The helmsman and crew settle down.

more so than when you are sailing downwind. Watching the sails, watching and feeling the wind, and handling the tiller with delicate skill are all techniques that require practice. Let's look at some of the step-by-step details of downwind sailing.

You do not need to have the centerboard down. You'll sail faster if it's up, because of the lowered resistance, but you must remember to put it down promptly when you change course and sail close-hauled.

Steering is more difficult than it is when you're sailing close-hauled. Very small changes with the tiller may be constantly needed to steer a straight course.

Your handling of the sheets is also different. Essentially, you trim the main boom so it is at right angles to the wind, as near as can be, and set the jibsheet so that the jib is full. However, this naturally depends on the course you're steering—as well as the trim of the mainsail.

You can sail downwind so that both the main and the jib are working on the same side (see the photograph on page 34). If you steer just a little farther away from the wind, the main will blanket the jib, which will then hang largely idle. This is the time to try sailing wing and wing (see the photograph on page 35). Let the trimmed jibsheet go, and bring the jib over to the opposite side, using the other jibsheet. With practice and attention you can perfect this delicately balanced maneuver.

Sailing straight downwind is fast and exhilarating because you know you have to be skillful, and, besides, it poses an element of potential danger.

Accidental jibing. The danger in sailing straight downwind is that you may have an *accidental jibe*. This happens when the wind catches the leeward side of the mainsail and sends the boom crashing over (watch your head!) to the opposite side of the boat. Having an accidental jibe, like getting in irons, is a result of inattention. *Don't jibe accidentally.* The boom's sudden swing to the other side can injure anyone in its way and also damage the rigging. Furthermore, in strong winds the careless jibe can heel the boat alarmingly, altering your steering so that you may lose control of the boat and let it swing broadside to the wind. This is called broaching, and it is a dangerous predicament to be in.

Some other points on sailing downwind.
- ▲ The boom should never be so far out that it touches the shrouds. The mainsail, though, may very well be against the shroud.
- ▲ Watch carefully for changes in the wind—these can lead to accidental jibes, even though you're sailing a straight course. A following sea can also push the boat around and cause an accidental jibe.
- ▲ Under many circumstances you'll make better time and have a slightly easier job of sailing if you tack downwind—alternately jibing from one very broad reach to the other, instead of sailing straight downwind wing and wing. The boat covers more distance, but often at a faster pace.

Sail trim errors. Besides getting the feeling for the proper way to do things, you can profit by knowing what not to do. Let's look at some problems, and how to avoid them.

▲ **Sagging sails.** If the mainsails and jib sag they don't work efficiently, and the halyards should be tightened. In a stiff breeze this can be difficult, unless the person at the helm luffs up and, during the few seconds of less pressure on the sail, the crew puts muscle into getting a tighter halyard.

▲ **Jibsheet hung up.** The weather sheet (the one not in use) may not have been loosened enough or may have caught on something so that the clew of the jib is held in toward the mast and the sail sets improperly. Free it.

▲ **Jib improperly trimmed.** After tacking, the crew may fail to get the jibsheet in properly. As the boat gets under way on her proper course, the main does all the work, and the jib is luffing. Let the jib out, and then pull it in until it fills properly.

▲ **Luffing main.** At times, in a stiff breeze, a boat will sail very well with the main luffing a trifle. But you have to know your boat and try out various settings to find this out. Improper trimming from inattention is simply sloppy.

▲ **Overtrimmed sails.** In a very light breeze, it is easy to haul in on the mainsheet, get the boom almost amidships, and trim the jib correspondingly hard. But the boat won't sail well. Try easing the sheets, and see how she picks up speed. Another point about overtrimming: it's often best not to pull the jib all the way in right after tacking; let the boat get moving again before trimming.

Back at the dock. Getting the boat back to her mooring or dock and lowering the sails is relatively simple. Picking up a mooring, landing at a dock, and dropping the sails are all best done by heading into the wind. Remember, a boat always stops sailing if you head her into the wind. What you have to practice is judging the distance she'll travel before stopping in the water so that you can put her bow right at the mooring or the dock just as she loses way.

Usually you drop your sails—jib first—*after* you tie up. But if you want to drop the jib while still sailing, here's the procedure. The person at the jib halyard looks to make sure the halyard is free to run. If it's been tucked away, he may have to overhaul it so that the line is loosely coiled and ready to run. Then the helmsman rounds up, and as the boat heads into the wind, the halyard is cast off the cleat and the jib comes down the stay. Sometimes, if the wind is blowing hard, the crew has to move forward and pull it down. Usually, at this point, it's a good idea to put a short piece of light line, called a *stop* or *gasket,* around the bunched-up jib.

After the boat is moored or tied up, the main is lowered; follow the same procedure as for the jib. The D-C's boom will drop into the cockpit, so don't sit under it.

If you're through sailing for the day, take the battens out of the mainsail. On a small boat, it's quick and easy to unfasten the halyard and take the sail off the boom, ready for the sail bag. On a larger cruising boat, you're more likely to furl the mainsail on the boom, so you should have sail stops ready.

To furl the mainsail, pull it out away from the mast, roll it into the foot section closest to the boom, and tie it atop the boom with the sail stops. To knot the sail stop, a slippery reef knot (see Chapter 9) is recommended, because it is always easy to untie.

COMMON ERRORS TO AVOID

If the jibsheet is not trimmed properly, the sail will luff (flap) and fail to do its job. The mainsail is wrinkled because the halyard is not tight.

If the jib sags it loses its efficiency. The remedy: take up on the jib halyard, so that the sail has a smooth airfoil shape, without wrinkles.

In light air, trimming the sheets hard slows the boat. The remedy: ease the sheets. Helmsman and crew should move to center.

If the windward jibsheet is too tight or is caught, as shown, the sail cannot fill properly and will only slow the boat.

5
FINE POINTS

In a thousand and one days of sailing, no two will be alike. And of all the variables you face, none is more unpredictable than the wind. Even if you have learned the basics of sailing under moderate, steady wind conditions, you will soon encounter days with light and fitful breezes that require a little extra knowledge and a lot of finesse.

SAILING IN LIGHT AIRS
Here are some pointers for light-air sailing.

▲ Both the main- and jibsheets should be

A cruising sloop heads out on a reach, with mainsail, spinnaker, and spinnaker staysail all set and drawing well.

eased just a bit compared to their settings for a stiff breeze. This gives the jib more shape, and the mainsail a better angle for light wind.

▲ Abrupt changes with the rudder slow the boat. This is true anytime, but if you are barely moving in the water, it is more critical. Steering in very light airs is a fingertip affair.

▲ The trim of the boat, that is, how she sits in the water, is critical too. If the crew's weight is too far aft or too far forward, the boat will be slowed. Sitting on the windward edge of the boat, as you might in a good breeze, will only give you a list to the opposite side if there's hardly any

breeze. This makes the sails inefficient
and slows the boat. If you move in the
boat, do it slowly; jumping about so that
the boat rocks also slows her.

▲ On some boats, particularly light ones,
the balance between sails, centerboard,
and rudder may be so delicate that a very
small adjustment in any of them or in
your weight distribution makes a big difference in how she sails.

▲ Downwind with any wind, but particularly in light air, try easing the boom
outhaul a bit to get more fullness in the
mainsail. (For sailing in a stiff wind you
tighten the outhaul.)

In general, when you are sailing around the
harbor in light air, the boat will be forgiving
of some small lapses in your technique and
timing. You can jibe easily, or you can tie the
boat up at the dock and let the sheets fly. You
can also start out from the dock with merely
a shove, even though the wind isn't right.

But be observant and wary. What works
one time in a calm won't work the following
weekend in a breeze.

SHORTENING SAIL

Under certain circumstances, reducing the
amount of sail you're carrying will make
sailing both easier and safer.

Sailing under the mainsail alone. You have
seen pictures of sailboats caught sailing in

Blitzen *has a reef in her mainsail and is sailing
"on her feet," whereas the sloop at left, whose
mainsail is also reefed, appears to be in a heavy
puff of wind that will soon hit* Blitzen, *heel her
over, and speed her along.*

74 FINE POINTS

When the breeze is light, it is possible to tie up to a dock with the sails up, as long as the sheets are eased and the skipper is close by and alert to any change in the strength of the wind.

storms, so you can appreciate full well one basic reason for shortening sail: high winds. There are also occasions when your convenience will be served by shortening sail, even in a light breeze. One example is when you are sailing through a harbor filled with moored boats. If you drop your jib and sail under the mainsail alone, you will gain several advantages:

▲ **Visibility.** Without the jib in the way you can see where you're going in crowded conditions.
▲ **Effortless sailing.** With only the mainsail

up, you can tack and jibe without handling jibsheets.
▲ **Room to move.** Especially on a large boat, if you get the jib down first and out of the way, there'll be room to move on the foredeck when anchoring or handling dock lines.

A second method of dropping the jib. Earlier, in Chapter 4 you learned to head into the wind to lower the sails. This is a good elementary technique, but if you are already on a broad reach or a run as you approach your home port, there's another way. Once you feel secure in downwind sailing, with your sense of wind direction sharp enough so that you won't get caught in an artificial jibe, you can have your crew drop the jib while it is in the lee of and being blanketed by the mainsail. There's no slatting about, no fuss. But if you're sailing solo, heading into the wind is still the best way to lower the jib. Dropping the mainsail, though, has to be done while the boat is headed into the wind, as you'll find out if you try it any other way.

There can be one disadvantage to sailing without the jib, however: not all sloops are easy to maneuver under mainsail alone.

Sailing under the jib alone. Most modern sloops can be sailed under the jib alone. If you are coming back across a body of water and find the wind has picked up, you *can* sail with the main up, of course, but on a broad reach it is hard work. Besides, the wind may continue to increase. So luff up, drop the mainsail, furl it so that it won't blow about, and sail home under the jib. On a reach, it's fast, comfortable, and easy. Whether you can tack with just the jib depends upon the par-

Inattention can spoil your day. This racing Lightning is risking an accidental jibe, not to mention a torn spinnaker, damaged rigging, and capsizing. If the spinnaker sheet is quickly cast off and the boat is held on course, all will be well. Gusty winds require careful attention.

ticular boat, and, to some extent, on your skill. Practice sailing with the jib alone before you actually need to do it.

REEFING

Reefing is a technique that is also best tried before a storm. With a small sloop your choices of when and how you tie in a reef are more limited than they are aboard a large cruising or racing boat.

Reefing the D-C. Reefing the mainsail of the D-C is best done before you start sailing. There are two reefing pendants built into the sail. The forward pendant is taken through the tack fitting, next to the mast, and tied down so that the place where it is attached to the sail becomes, in effect, the sail's new tack. Similarly, the leech pendant is tied down to the outer end of the boom. Your spare line, from the clew, is laced through the reef grommets in the belly of the sail and around the sail—not around the boom—to make as tight a parcel of the sail as possible; the line is then secured at the forward end of the boom.

Reefing larger boats. A larger boat sometimes has reef points—small lengths of

WHAT TO DO WHEN YOU CAPSIZE

Get onto the centerboard and use your weight to slowly lift the sail out of the water. On a larger boat take the sail down first.

As the boat rights herself, climb back in, taking care not to bring the boat over so fast she capsizes again.

line sewn through the sail where the D-C's reef grommets are. These are tied around the bolt rope of the sail, with a reef knot used each time. Other boats have roller reefing, in which the boom is turned so that the sail wraps around it. A strong, well-trained crew can roll in a reef while still sailing. But nowadays, most big boats have a simpler system, known as jiffy reefing, that is very similar to the system found on the D-C.

SAILING IN STRONG WINDS

As you have already noticed, not every departure from standard good practice is in itself bad. When you learned the step-by-step procedures to follow in a moderate wind, the right thing to do for close-hauled sailing was to trim the jib and main well in. You learned to steer very close to the wind, without quite luffing. But let's say some gusts of very strong wind come along. A good solution in this case is to point higher, to momentarily luff up into the wind. You can do this with your tiller, without any adjustment of the sails, and it will lessen the heeling force of the wind. Let's say the strong winds continue to the point where you're tired of having the rail almost under the water all the time. Ease the mainsheet a bit, so the main is just luffing, and you will sail more "on your feet," or less heeled over, and probably just as fast. On a large racing or cruising boat you'd probably shift to a smaller jib in this situation.

Capsizing. You should also know what to do when you have been careless or when a puff is too strong to handle and you get laid over on your side. This is called a *knockdown*, and

The boat should be headed into the wind, and you have to keep your balance as you take the tiller. Sit on the high side.

Off and sailing again! Knowing what to do if you capsize is essential, but knowing how to avoid capsizing is even more valuable.

often the puff passes and the boat simply rights itself. But if you get knocked down too far and too much water comes in over the side, you'll go over to stay, and that's *capsizing.*

Don't panic. The boat won't sink if it has built-in flotation, and if you stay close to it and hang on, neither will you. You may have to act quickly to keep unattached items from floating away, but don't ever swim very far from the boat.

All board boats—such as the Sunfish, Phantom, and Laser—and most small centerboarders with good flotation can be righted by an agile crew after capsizing (see photographs, pages 78 and 79). To right such a boat, swim around to the centerboard or dagger board and stand on it, using your weight to right the boat. But be careful not to

capsize the boat again while climbing back aboard. Some centerboarders, but not the D-C, will have to be bailed out after they're upright again. For this reason, it's a good precaution to keep a bailer aboard and to tie it down. Larger boats, even those with flotation, may be too unwieldy to get back upright without hauling down the sails as they lie in the water. This is not an easy job, but it can be done.

In general, capsizing is preventable. If you are sailing in puffy winds, hold the mainsheet in your hand ready for instant release instead of cleating it. Cleating the mainsheet is the most common cause of capsizing. An uncontrolled jibe in a strong wind can also make you capsize. So can getting in irons in puffy winds and a lack of agility in distributing the weight of skipper and crew.

PROPER EQUIPMENT

As you've learned, a great deal of the proper technique for each kind of sailing consists of preparation: having the right gear at hand and knowing exactly what steps to take in any situation. In a way, all good sailing boils down to good preparation.

Among the fine points of sailing, therefore, is having the proper equipment on board. That is, you and your boat should always be prepared *for any conditions you'll encounter*. If you're sailing on a three-mile lake, you don't need a sea anchor or electronic navigating equipment, but it would be sensible to have a knife, some waterproof tape, and some light line for making small repairs. In any case, you must always have the safety equipment required by law (see page 143). If, on any size boat, you are going to tie up to a dock for a few hours, you will also need adequate dock lines and probably fenders (see Chapter 7 on boat handling). If you're sailing on a large body of water, you need a chart, a compass, and the knowledge to use them. All these are basics, but they are violated every week by boating novices who try to exceed the capabilities of themselves and their equipment.

For instance, there are hundreds of thousands of small boats out on the water without anchors. Most of the time, an anchor is not needed. But if you are becalmed, or carried by currents to places you don't want to go, an adequate anchor and anchor line are necessities. See Chapter 7 for information on anchors and anchoring.

For safety's sake, you should make your own equipment checklist, based on the type of boat you sail, the waters you sail in, and the kind of sailing you plan to do.

Heaving to in normal weather. There are many times when you may want to stop, or heave to, while out on the water. You may want to stop and eat lunch, or have a swim, or practice pulling someone who has gone overboard back into the boat. Rod Stephens recommends this simple method for heaving to in normal weather in a small boat: (1) drop the headsail and let the mainsail luff freely; (2) guy the boom forward by tying it with a line to the bow cleat or stem fitting, easing and adjusting the mainsheet in such a way that the boom is held securely out, perpendicular to the boat; (3) push the tiller to leeward. With this set-up the mainsail acts like a weathervane while the rudder keeps the mainsail from filling, and the keel or centerboard prevents sideways motion. The boat should remain virtually stationary with a minimum of motion as the sail alternately fills and luffs, sending the boat ahead at very slow speed.

LEARNING BY OBSERVING

A smart sailor picks up better ways of doing things by watching others. (Making awkward mistakes of your own is also an effective way to learn.) If you notice, for example, on a sparkling sunny day while you're still in the harbor that a much larger boat is coming in with a reef tied in the mainsail and the crew in foul-weather gear, you'll know what to prepare for. And you'll stow your lunch and sweater up under the foredeck where they will be protected from the inevitable spray.

In the regular rhythm of sailing there are scores of situations that call for a look ahead. Following are two examples.

If you are on a cruising boat and you're

A Columbia 22 noses up to a beach on a windless afternoon after a stern anchor has been put down. Her mainsail is still up, and it poses no problem unless the wind comes up.

planning to drop and furl the mainsail, make sure the sail stops are put in place a couple of minutes ahead of time. Place the stops over the boom and under the bolt rope (on a rig where this can be done), so that when you start furling the sail, everything is at hand.

Learn to read the markers in areas where you sail often. For example, at the entrance to a particular harbor, one buoy may serve as a signpost by the way it leans with the current, indicating its direction and strength. From observing the buoy, you can safely plan your entrance to the harbor each time you enter it.

This habit of constant observation of the things going on around you—wind, current, other boats—applies just as importantly to your own boat, particularly to the set of the sails. Remember that wind direction is almost never constant, and that sometimes little normal shifts back and forth become big ones. Sometimes, if you're not careful

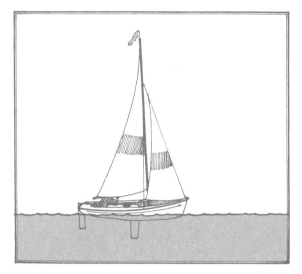

When sailing close-hauled, keep the centerboard down to prevent the boat from making leeway. Note the wind pennant at the masthead.

When the wind is aft and you are running, raise the centerboard to increase speed; the board is not needed to prevent leeway.

when sailing along on a fixed course with the sails trimmed, let's say close-hauled, you may actually find yourself sailing on a reach if the wind shifts. If you haven't noticed the shift and your sails are too far in, your boat will poke along sluggishly, a sure sign of a helmsman who's not keeping his eye on the telltales. The remedy is to ease the sheets to pick up speed.

Sailing by the lee. Another situation in which your close observation of the wind is especially important is when you steer downwind so far away from the wind that it comes over the side the boom is on. In other words, the stern has already passed through the wind, but the sail, being way out, hasn't. This is called sailing *by the lee*. You can sail this way on purpose, especially if you're racing or trying to get around a buoy without having to jibe, but a beginner can do it inadvertently, and sailing by the lee is a very short step from an accidental jibe.

Above all, develop the habit of inspecting your boat constantly for flaws of any kind—from improperly set sails and faulty rigging to parts that need fixing, lubrication or replacement.

WEATHER HELM AND LEE HELM

One nuance of sailing that you should become aware of after you've mastered the basics is the matter of *weather helm* and *lee helm.*

To illustrate, let's take the D-C out on the water, while there's a light to moderate breeze blowing. We'll trim the main and jib so she's sailing close to the wind—it takes just a fin-

When sailing in shallow water or approaching a beach, lift the centerboard and, if possible on your boat, the rudder blade.

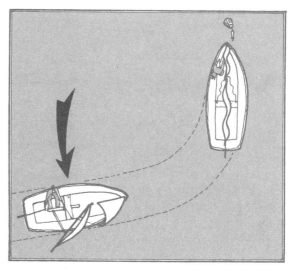

When rounding up to a mooring buoy, let the boat coast into the wind, with the centerboard down for greater stability.

gertip on the tiller. Take your hand off the tiller, and notice what happens. If the boat slowly steers herself upwind until she begins to luff, she is said to have a slight weather helm. When sailing, you naturally correct for this with the tiller by keeping it slightly to windward of the center line. If the boat has a tendency to gradually bear off, until she is at right angles to the wind, you'd say she had a lee helm.

A designer normally plans a boat so that she will have a very slight weather helm. Part of the reason for this is that it makes the boat easier to steer well if there is a slight "feel" to the helm and part is that it is safer to have a boat that will round up into the wind—and stop—should the helmsman lose control of the tiller.

A boat is normally rigged to keep the qualities her designer intended. However, if the sails are not standard, or the mast is raked forward by overtightening the jibstay, she could develop a little lee helm. At times the position of the centerboard and the weight distribution of the crew as well as variations in the rigging adjustments can also affect the helm of some boats. Make sure the boat you sail shows a little weather helm; if she doesn't, take steps to set things right.

This chapter has only begun to explore the fine points of sailing, for every boat and rig has its own particular fine points, and every body of water guards its own secrets. From now until the day you come ashore for good, you'll be learning the fine points—refining and perfecting your knowledge and skills. And that's what makes sailors who are experts and who love the sport.

6

OTHER BOATS, OTHER RIGS

The variety of rigs that sailors have devised for moving boats through water seems almost infinite. From Arab dhows to Chinese junks, from South Sea proas to experimental multihulled vessels with sails that resemble airplane wings on end, these creations are beautiful to look at and intriguing to discuss. But none is more glorious than the square-rigger, an early nineteenth-century version of which is illustrated under a crowd of sail and a maze of rigging in the old print at left.

In today's sailing world even small boats try for the grace of the great square-rigged ships of the early 1800s—but the sailors have an easier and safer life.

All these vessels are part of the enduring romance of the sea, and, in some ways, they are all related to the more familiar boats you see and sail aboard. What follows is a look at various kinds of hulls and rigging arrangements.

So far we have concentrated on one class of boat, the D-C, to simplify the process of learning the basics of sailing. And because the D-C is similar to scores of other small sloops used for instruction at sailing schools and in yacht-club sailing programs, the same information generally holds true for all of them. However, the variations in hull and sail plans of larger boats are numerous enough to require some explanation.

HULL DESIGNS

For all practical purposes there are two basic types of hulls: those with centerboards, such as the D-C, and those with fixed keels.

Centerboard hulls. The simplest type of centerboard is called a *dagger board*, which slides down through a slot in the hull. It is inexpensive to construct and suitable for the very small, light boats carried in station wagons or stowed on the cabin tops of cruising boats. Alternatively, the centerboard may be housed in a centerboard trunk, pivoted on a pin, and controlled by the centerboard pendant, as in the D-C. While this arrangement is more complex, it offers more flexibility. It also provides protection when you are sailing in shallow water: if the board hits the bottom it bounces up in the same manner as the D-C's rudder blade.

Centerboard boats depend for stability on the shape of the hull and the shifting weight of the crew. They tend to be broad of beam, and their hulls are designed so that they resist heeling beyond a certain point. They're light, lively, and responsive.

With some exceptions, centerboard boats are smaller than keelboats. They're well suited for day sailing, for hauling out on beaches, and for getting onto trailers.

UNDERWATER PROFILES FOR A VARIETY OF PURPOSES

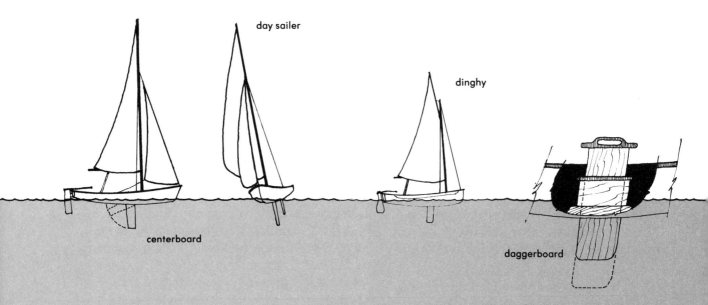

Spry day sailers have light hulls and, usually, a centerboard and broad beam for stability.

Small dinghies have daggerboards for their light weight and simple construction.

They're extremely popular in shallow waters because they can be sailed with the board half up, when necessary.

Keel hulls. The characteristics of a keelboat are easily understood. The fixed keel in most cases is a structural part of the boat; it not only provides lateral resistance, as does the centerboard, but its weight also helps maintain the stability of the boat. A keelboat can take a knockdown from a puff of wind because the weight of the keel will help her right herself. If she has a watertight cockpit and the hatches are closed, she won't sink from being knocked down, which makes her best suited for off-shore sailing.

There are exceptions, of course. Some seagoing boats have been designed with centerboards, and a good many day sailers have keels. Many of the latter have deep, thin keels, called *fin keels,* that provide the light and responsive behavior of high-performance centerboarders.

In general, however, it is fair to say that keelboats are heavier and less lively than centerboarders. This means that although they are sailed much the same way, their hulls behave differently. A light centerboarder is quick to accelerate, for instance, whereas a heavy keelboat gains more momentum, so

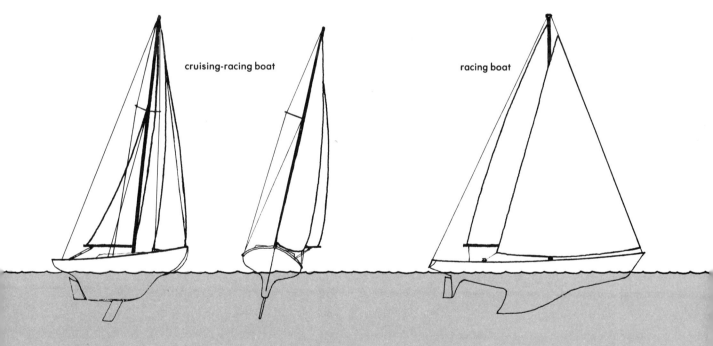

cruising-racing boat

racing boat

Some cruising-racing boats have a centerboard inside the keel, for shoal water areas.

Large racing boats are designed to reduce the wetted surface area of the keel for greater speed.

that when you come about she carries her way longer as you turn through the wind. Similarly, when rounding up into the wind to approach a mooring or dock, the keelboat glides several boat lengths before stopping, while a centerboarder loses her way more quickly, and you miss your target if you bring her up from too far away. Because of her weight and design, a keelboat is usually more "comfortable" in rough water than a bouncy centerboarder. (This is like saying a limousine is more comfortable than a sports car; some people prefer the sports-car ride.)

Keelboats with long keels have more directional stability than centerboarders or keelboats with short, deep keels, and they require less attention to steer in a straight line—just as long skis hold their track better than short skis. On the other hand, they are harder to turn, and because they often have more underwater surface causing friction with the water, they tend to be slower.

Designers develop endless variations of keel shapes and rudder positions in their search for racing speed and other characteristics. As with everything in naval archi-

UNDERWATER PROFILES FOR A VARIETY OF PURPOSES

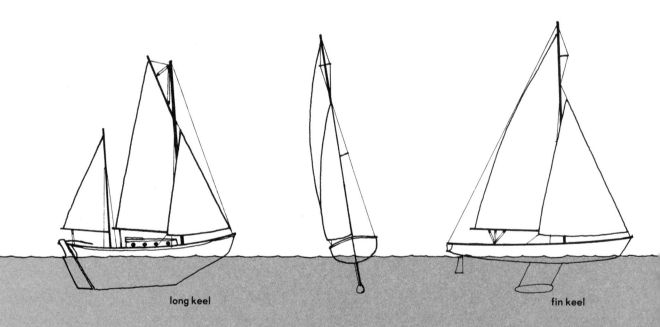

long keel

fin keel

Long keels on cruising boats give directional stability and handling ease.

Fin keels make for speed by cutting down on the wetted surface.

tecture, a gain in one aspect may bring about a disadvantage in another. People who use their boats mainly for cruising tend to prefer easy sailing to the gain in speed achieved by high-performance designs.

Other hull shapes. Several alternate hull designs provide solutions to problems such as shoal water, stability, and speed. Europeans, far more than Americans, favor small cruising boats with twin keels that angle out from the hull. These boats can sail in shallow water, and they are useful in areas with extreme tides because they can sit upright on the bottom when the tide goes out. They can also rest on their own keels when hauled out in the off-season.

A compromise that has worked well in some designs, such as the famous ocean racer, *Finisterre,* is the keel-centerboarder. In this type of hull, the keel, which is less deep than usual, houses a large metal centerboard that can be lowered to increase the boat's lateral resistance when sailing on the wind.

Finally, there are catamarans, which are twin-hulled, and trimarans, which have a

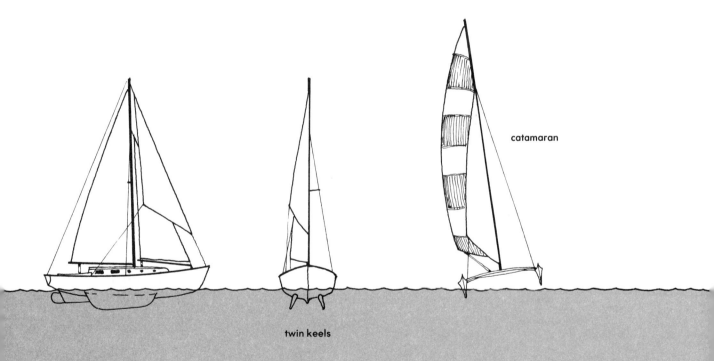

twin keels

catamaran

Twin keels on cruising boats are seen mostly in Europe in shallow-water areas.

Double-hull catamarans are fast because they create little friction against the water.

main hull and two outboard stabilizing hulls. These vessels, derived from ancient designs, are enjoying increasing popularity. Their unusually wide beam gives them enormous stability that enables them to carry more sail for their weight than monohulls and thus attain extremely high speeds under many conditions.

SAIL PLANS

You can be glad that today you don't have to stand on the foot ropes of a square-rigger, hanging onto the yardarm and clawing at wet canvas, and you can be grateful for the ways that naval architects, sailmakers, boatbuilders, and riggers have simplified sailing rigs in the last century.

The simplest of all boats to sail is the modern sailing dinghy (not to be confused with some racing dinghies such as the International 14, which are a little more elab-

orate). Most are *catboats,* with one sail and therefore only one sheet to tend. You can come about by moving only the tiller. You need to duck as the boom swings over, and you may need to shift your weight if there's a breeze and the boat is heeling.

Many small catboats are used as tenders or for "off-the-beach" sport.

Single-masted rigs. The *sloop,* with its basic rig of main and jib, is a design of great efficiency. Those who know aerodynamics can explain how the two sails work together to do more work than the sum of their separate efforts. Of the two sails, the jib is perhaps the most fascinating. Jibs range in size from a tiny storm, or spitfire, jib, at one extreme, to a huge overlapping Genoa at the other. Although the constant search for greater speed has led to great developments in the design and trim of jibs, one old-fashioned variation

A SAMPLING OF SAIL PLANS AND WHY THEY'RE POPULAR

marconi sail

lug sail

gaff-rigged sail

The modern marconi sail on the small catboat at left is easy to rig, while a lug sail rig with its short mast (center) that can be tucked in the bottom of the boat is popular for dinghies. An older-type catboat (right) uses hoops to hold the sail to the mast and a gaff at the top of the sail.

still has a unique advantage: the club-footed jib, whose foot may be on a club or boom. The advantage of this jib is that it has only one sheet, so no one needs to tend the sheet when the boat comes about.

Some single-masted boats, usually cruising boats, are rigged with a self-tending foresail (also known as a forestaysail) *and* a jib. When shortening sail, the jib can be doused first and when carrying a full sail, the efficiency is fairly good. Many boats with this rig have a bowsprit that extends out over the bow. In the United States these boats are usually called *cutters*, although the word cutter has a number of other meanings when applied to boats and ships. Even those who study such matters do not always agree: some experts argue that if a boat's single mast is stepped more than one-third of the way aft from the bow, it is a cutter, whether it carries a single- or double-headsail rig. The drawing on page 92 shows what some authorities would call a cutter rig.

In contrast to the simple rigging of a D-C, the cutter has a number of additional parts, most of which are normally found on larger boats.

Backstay. The backstay, for example, helps support the mast and takes the pressure of downwind sailing.

Topping lift. Boats with a larger boom also require special support for the boom, even

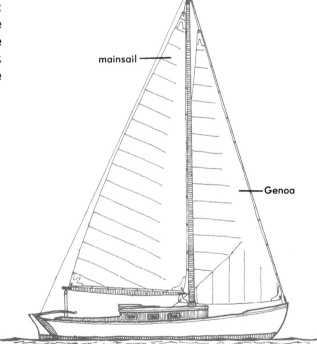

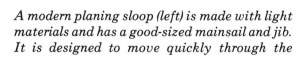

A modern planing sloop (left) is made with light materials and has a good-sized mainsail and jib. It is designed to move quickly through the *water. A typical small cruising sloop (right) is more heavily built and may carry several sizes of jibs for varying wind conditions.*

OTHER BOATS, OTHER RIGS 91

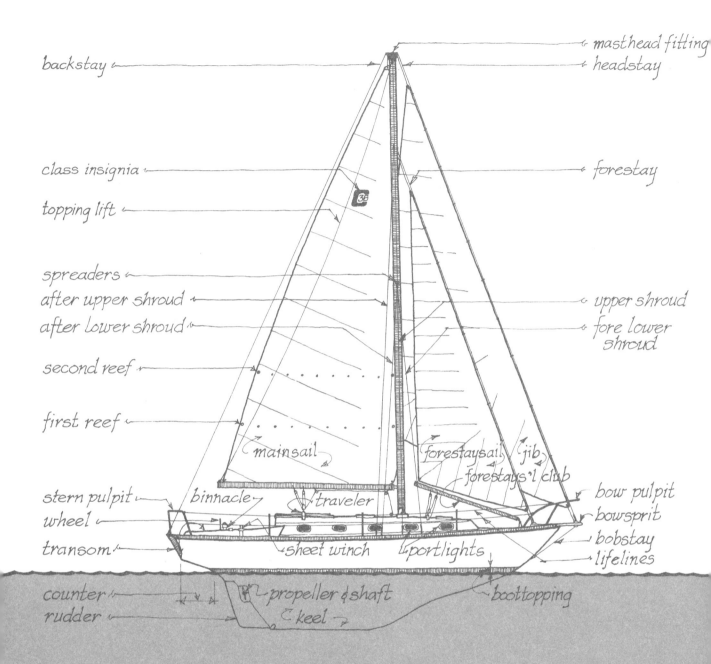

backstay

masthead fitting
headstay

class insignia

forestay

topping lift

spreaders
after upper shroud
after lower shroud

upper shroud
fore lower shroud

second reef

first reef

mainsail

forestaysail   jib
forestays'l club

stern pulpit
binnacle   traveler
bow pulpit

wheel
bowsprit

transom
sheet winch   portlights
bobstay
lifelines

counter
propeller & shaft
boottopping

rudder
keel

A typical cruising boat with mainsail and double headsails has many more rigging and construction details than the simple day sailer; for example, there are the bowsprit, permanent backstay, sheetwinch, keel, and propeller. Some details, such as the transom, are found on almost any boat or ship; others, such as the bobstay, appear only with a bowsprit.

when the mainsail is not hoisted. This is provided by an adjustable topping lift, sometimes made of wire rope but more often of Dacron line that is run through a block. The block is usually placed on the outer end of the boom or near the top of the mast. The latter arrangement is convenient for making adjustments because the lift comes down the mast, but it means extra windage when you're sailing. To avoid this, a piece of shock cord can be run from just above the middle of the lift to a thimble spliced onto the backstay, then down to the stern. That arrangement keeps the topping lift from fouling the sail, and the elasticity of the lift permits the boom to be well out without raising it too much when the boat is sailing downwind.

Shrouds. Note that the cutter has more than one shroud; this is customary. The lower shrouds, two on each side, take a lot of the strain of sailing and, in effect, change the sideways pressure on the mast to a pull against the chain plates. The upper shrouds, one on each side, go over a spreader, and the resulting engineering geometry helps keep the mast from bending.

Halyards and sheets. The halyards and sheets on larger boats naturally have the same functions as those on the D-C. However, the number of lines increases with the number of sails. There are sheets for the foresail as well as for the jib. Yawls, ketches, and schooners with more sails merely have more halyards and sheets, all appropriately named.

Spinnaker. If the boat carries a spinnaker, a large sail used for downwind sailing, a few more terms are apropos. The spinnaker has a sheet attached to its free corner that functions like the sheet on a jib. It also has a pole lift that works like a topping lift to keep the spinnaker pole from dropping when it shouldn't. Each end of the spinnaker pole is supported by a guy: the forward guy is used to pull the pole forward and hold it down, and the after guy is used to pull the pole aft. When one is taken up, the other must be correspondingly eased, and when you jibe, the pole is turned—so that what was a guy becomes a sheet, and what was the sheet becomes the after guy.

Handling a spinnaker is a skill that comes slowly, usually from helping experienced crew members set it, jibe it, and take it in. There are a number of ways to handle the pole in a jibe, as well as terms to describe it.

If you're watching a boat that is sailing under spinnaker, check to see if the pole is horizontal or cocked upward. If it's horizontal, the spinnaker is set properly to get maximum use of the sail area. But if the pole slants upward, someone isn't tending to his job. When you graduate to using a spinnaker, you should be able to control the pole with ease, using the forward guy and the pole lift. This information is not intended to teach you spinnaker handling, but it will enable you to watch others with a little more understanding.

Downhaul. A downhaul is also common on large boats. There are two kinds: one rigged to enable a small crew to lower the sail in a strong wind, and another, more common type that is attached to the boom at the mast and is used to get the lower luff wrinkles out of the mainsail.

Shock cord. One of the most versatile and useful items of rigging on many boats is shock cord, which is elastic and resembles braided line. Shock cord has already been mentioned in connection with keeping the topping lift out of the roach of the mainsail. It is also used to fasten sail covers and quick-furling setups. A short piece of shock cord makes a quick temporary stop or gasket on a jib to keep it from blowing about. Some skippers fasten a couple of pieces of shock cord across the foredeck so that one person getting the jib down in a blow can tuck it under the cords in a hurry without having

MANY SAILS FOR MANY CONDITIONS

The full sail plan on the typical cruising sloop at right would also serve for cruiser-racers, which often carry on board four or five headsails of different sizes and various light sails to meet varying wind conditions.

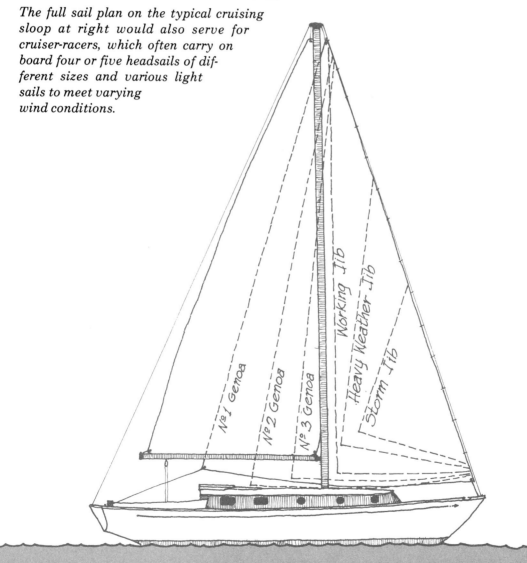

Nº 1 Genoa
Nº 2 Genoa
Nº 3 Genoa
Working Jib
Heavy Weather Jib
Storm Jib

too much sail to handle. Short pieces of shock cord are often made up with toggles for holding coiled dock lines or extra sheets. Because shock cord can't be spliced, brass or plastic clamps are usually used to keep the ends from unraveling or to make an eye in one end.

Two-masted rigs. There are more variations in design to be seen among two-masted yachts. Yawls and ketches, for example, both have a mizzenmast, or aftermast, that is shorter than the mainmast. But the mizzenmast of a ketch is generally larger than that of a yawl. The major difference between

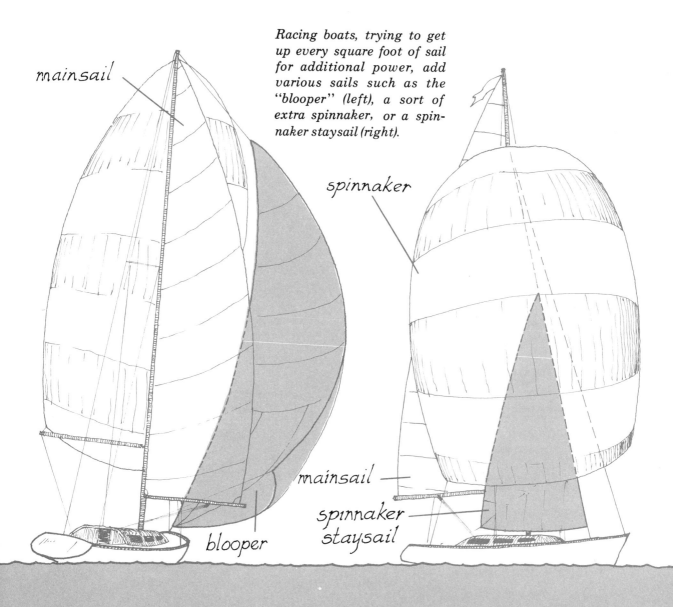

mainsail

Racing boats, trying to get up every square foot of sail for additional power, add various sails such as the "blooper" (left), a sort of extra spinnaker, or a spinnaker staysail (right).

spinnaker

mainsail

blooper

spinnaker
staysail

the two boats, however, is in the location of the smaller mast—behind the rudder post for yawls, and ahead of the rudder post for ketches. Both yawls and ketches can set various combinations of sails, and, in some ways, they are both easier to handle than sloops of the same sail area because the main can be dropped and the vessel can sail under jib and mizzen alone. These boats can also add to their sail area with a staysail set to the top of the mizzenmast. The tradeoff, however, is that there are more halyards, topping lifts, and sheets to take care of and handle.

Another two-masted rig that is still popular, if mainly for nostalgic reasons, is the *schooner,* although few are being built today. Schooners are usually thought of as having a foremast shorter than the mainmast, but this definition applies only when the vessel is two-masted, as with most schooner yachts. Schooners with three or more masts—even as many as seven—were often built for commercial use, and their masts were usually the same height. In the days of commercial sail, schooners could be sailed with smaller crews than ships, with square sails that required many hands to shift and trim them.

Within the basic two-masted rigs there are also many sail-plan variations, such as the wishbone ketch or the staysail schooner. On both of these boats the staysails are com-

MANY SAILS FOR MANY CONDITIONS

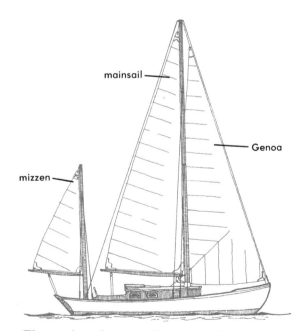

The yawl, with its small mizzen behind the tiller, offers a flexible sail plan.

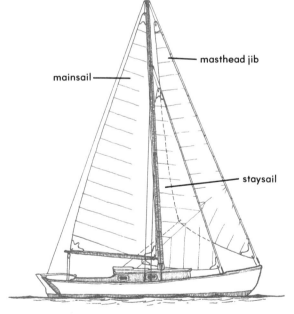

On a boat with a double headsail rig, the sail area can be shortened by dropping the jib.

bined in different configurations to produce exotic rigs that have enthusiastic adherents. One particularly beautiful rig is the *brigantine,* which is square-rigged on the foremast and fore-and-aft rigged on the mainmast. A few yachts of this type are still to be seen.

Some ancient rigs, such as the full-battened Chinese junk, have modern multihull counterparts. If you keep watching, you'll see new ideas, too.

For the first third of this century, books about sailing customarily offered the reader advice on the type of rig and hull that could be designed by one's own naval architect. Today most boats are stock- or semistock-built. Those that are custom-built tend to be designed for speed, efficiency, and ease of handling for a small crew. Thus, extra masts, jib booms, and gaffs, together with their fascinating hardware, are mainly found only on older boats. One exception is the bowsprit, which is still adding grace to some new boats because it is so useful for handling an anchor.

Marconi vs. gaff rig. Most sailboats today are Marconi-rigged, that is—their mainsails (and mizzensails) are triangular, with the long side at the luff. But before this design was introduced in the 1920s, yachts were gaff-rigged; their mainsails were four-sided, with a shorter luff and a top edge stretched

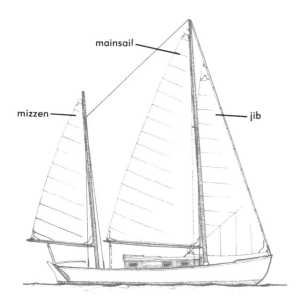

The ketch is another variation of a divided sail plan. Its mizzen is larger than a yawl's.

A schooner, with a marconi main and gaff foresail, is graceful, but not efficient.

out by a spar called a gaff. This graceful rig can still be seen occasionally, particularly on catboats, but it is decidedly old-fashioned.

The Marconi sail, also called a Bermudian or jib-headed sail, is more efficient, not only because it has one less spar, less weight aloft, and simpler running rigging, but also because the long luff is where most of the sail's work is done when a boat is close-hauled or reaching. (The Marconi rig, incidentally, got its name apparently because the tall mast that supports it, with its relatively complex standing rigging, reminded yachtsmen of a wireless transmitting tower, which in turn called to mind the inventor of wireless, Guglielmo Marconi.)

Handling more complicated rigs. If you get into sailing on an elaborately rigged boat you'll have to adapt to some variations in the rigging. Here are some short pointers to keep in mind.

On Genoa jibs of different sizes, the sheets lead to different places on the deck or rail, where they go through lead blocks, and then lead to a winch. (Sometimes the sheets lead outside the shrouds, sometimes inside.) Usually the blocks or fairleads are on tracks, so they can be adjusted fore and aft. Each jib will have its own settings on these tracks, and a good crewman will learn the positions by heart.

Getting a sheet onto a winch requires a

HISTORIC RIGS WITH MODERN USES

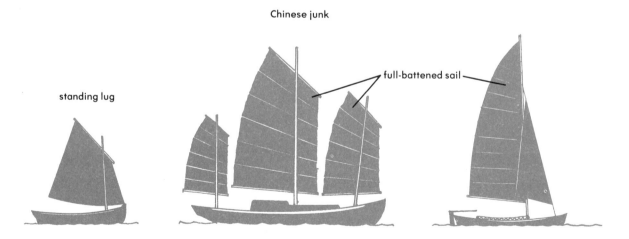

Centuries-old rigs, such as the standing lug (left) and the full-battened Chinese junk (center) are still in use today. Sails similar to a junk's are among the "modern" ways to get speed.

knack. You wrap the sheet in clockwise turns around the winch drum, and then pull, or tail, the sheet while the winch is cranked. Do not put too many turns on the drum, or the turns will ride over one another. If the wind is strong, it takes strong measures to get the overrides unfouled. In light winds or on small boats, one person can handle both the sheet and the winch handle. On larger boats, especially when the wind is strong, it takes two persons—one on the tail, the other working the handle to pull in a sheet. Like much of sailing, it takes teamwork.

The aftermost sail on a square-rigged ship (right) was called the spanker.

This brigantine carries a combination of fore-and-aft triangular sails as well as square sails, which are still found on some training vessels.

7

BOAT
HANDLING

To maneuver a sailboat in restricted or crowded waters; to anchor her safely; to bring her alongside docks or other boats in uncertain currents and strong winds; to handle her under sail or under power so that she, the people aboard, and other craft are safe—all this is truly an art.

This paragraph, paraphrased from the opening of Holloway Frost's excellent little book *On a Destroyer's Bridge,* aptly describes what the skipper of almost any size or type of sailboat needs to know about boat handling. Once you've learned the

---

Handling a sailboat under power in restricted space is a delicate job.

basics of sailing a boat, then you have to learn the skills—anchoring, steering, docking—needed to handle the boat in all normal situations.

Anchoring. Anchoring is a typical procedure used on a cruising boat that's stopping for the night in a sheltered harbor. This is what happens on board as she enters the harbor. The skipper carefully checks the chart and takes the safe channel at the entrance to the harbor. The chart tells him where the bottom is clay, sand, rocks, or mud, and how deep the water is in different parts of the harbor. He chooses an area where the water is deep enough for his keel, even at low tide. If he can, he selects the windward side of the harbor, under the lee of the land, where there will be less wave motion during the night, ensuring more comfort aboard and less strain on the anchor. He makes sure that other boats are not too close, and rechecks the chart for hidden underwater obstructions.

Anchoring a Cruising Sailboat. *To anchor, the skipper finds a spot with plenty of room, heads into the wind or current, and the crew drops anchor (1). The wind, current, or power takes the boat back, and the crew lets out line and snubs it to dig the anchor in; the anchor chain should also rest fully on the bottom (2). If the holding ground is poor or the wind is strong, the scope may be five times the depth of water, or seven times if a storm is due (3). After again checking that the anchor is not dragging and that other boats are not too near, the skipper and crew can relax (4).*

Anchoring under power. If the skipper intends to negotiate the harbor under power, he rounds up into the wind where there is room to maneuver, and then lowers his sails. The mainsail is furled, and the jib is either tied so it is out of the way or removed and put in its bag.

Then with the boat under power, the skipper takes her slowly toward the anchorage area. The crew gets the anchor ready, freeing it from the chocks that held it secure while sailing. The anchor line is at-

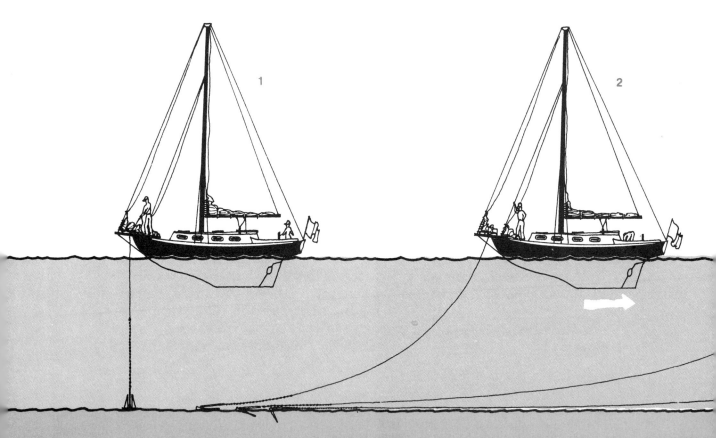

tached to the anchor with a *shackle,* a U-shaped metal fitting, and the line is overhauled, if necessary, to get rid of any kinks and snarls.

As the boat nears the desired spot, the skipper slows her still more. He takes the boat to a place several boat lengths beyond where he wants to lie when anchored and lets her come to a stop in the water. The crew drops the anchor over the bow (it shouldn't be thrown), taking care that the line is not fouled around the anchor as it goes down. The skipper slowly backs the boat, keeping her head to the wind.

As the anchor reaches bottom, the crew notes the depth (anchor lines are often conveniently marked at six-foot intervals) and lets out the anchor line slowly as the boat backs down. When the amount of line run out is from three to four times the depth of the water, the crew snubs the line on a cleat or bitt. The boat continues in reverse, and the anchor digs in.

Both the skipper and the crew check that the anchor is holding, not dragging, and when they're satisfied that all is well, the anchor line is cleated down and the motor turned off. The boat is now anchored.

There are some variations on the anchoring procedure, however.

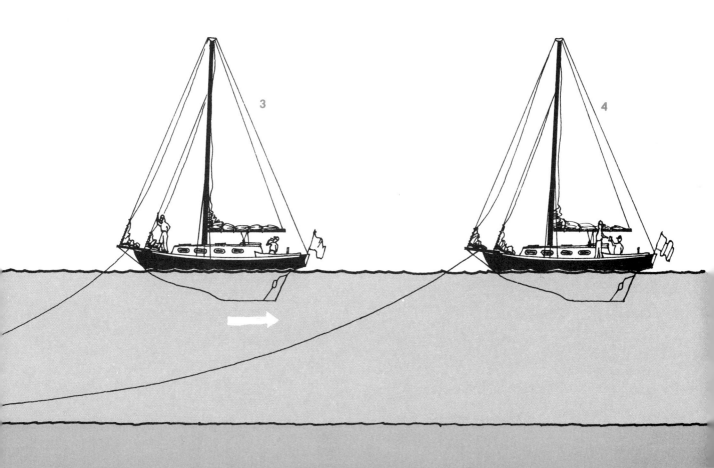

If storm conditions exist or are feared, or the rise and fall of the tide is extreme, the *scope*—the amount of anchor line out in relation to the depth of the water—should be increased to five, six, or even seven times the depth of the water. A look at the drawings reveals the obvious explanation for this: the more horizontal the anchor line, the more the anchor will tend to dig in. A too-short line with a heavy vertical strain on it will pull the anchor up and out.

Most sailors put a short length of chain, six feet perhaps, between the anchor and the anchor line. The chain serves three purposes: the chain's weight helps keep the pull of the anchor line horizontal; it prevents damage to the rope from sharp rocks on the bottom; the chain is almost self-washing, so a dirty anchor line won't be hauled back into the boat if it has been on a mud bottom.

A day sailer that is seldom anchored doesn't need any chain and won't have a very large anchor. However, it is always a

Getting the anchor up, once the line is shortened, is usually easy, but after a long blow it may be necessary to use engine power and move forward slowly.

A permanent mooring relies more on the weight and shape of its mushroom anchor than on scope to avoid dragging, but adequate chain is required, especially if tides run high.

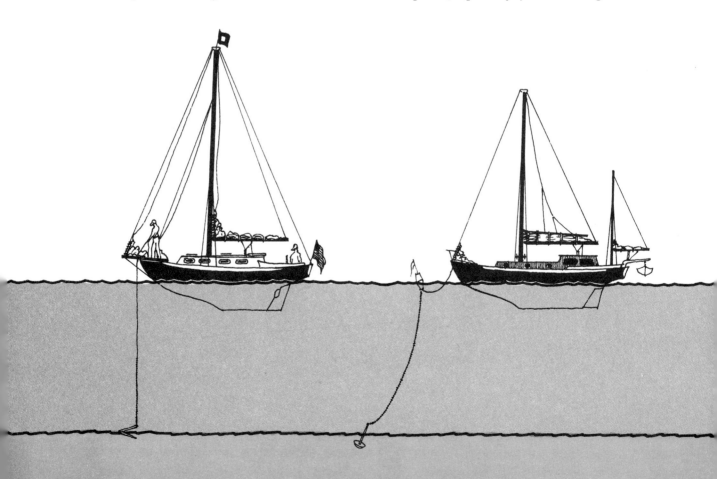

good idea to have some kind of anchor aboard, attached to its line and ready to go.

If it turns out that the anchor does not hold where it is dropped, or that the boat is not in an ideal position after all, it is necessary to pull up the anchor and try again.

If the wind changes later so that the boat lies in a different direction, be sure to check that the anchor is holding when the boat pulls in the new direction, and that the boat has not swung too close to another boat, a dock, or a rock.

Anchoring under sail. It is also possible for a cruising boat to sail to its anchorage, drop the sails and anchor, and let the wind take the boat back to dig in the anchor. This takes more skill, at least some wind, and perhaps more maneuvering room; but when it's done right, anchoring under sail is a very seamanlike operation.

Which anchor? A cruising boat normally carries an everyday anchor and, in addition, a storm anchor, which is very heavy; the two are not necessarily of the same type. Different types of anchors do their work of attaching a boat to the bottom in different ways. A design that digs well into mud won't always do well on a hard bottom. So your choice of anchor depends on what kind of bottom you are likely to encounter when you sail.

Sailors mostly use three types of anchor: the yachtman's (also known as the Herreshoff), the Danforth, and the plow (see diagrams, page 106). The plow anchor is hard to stow because of its shape, but if your boat has a bowsprit, the plow will stow very nicely underneath it. The plow holds very well, and also tends to come up clean after being in mud, clay, clam shells, and other debris. The Danforth stows flat, has great holding power for its weight, and is probably the most popular anchor of all with cruising people. The Herreshoff needs less scope to hold firm; but it also seems to be losing popularity. The Bruce anchor, a new British design, has no moving parts, is lightweight, and holds as well and with less scope than the heavier plows and Danforths. However, it is hard to stow on a small boat. Some anchor patents have expired and imitations are appearing; however, most knowledgeable sailors prefer the original proven designs.

Obviously the design of an anchor determines its holding power under differing conditions, but its weight and size are also important. The bigger and heavier it is, the better an anchor holds. Some anchors made of high-tensile steel are larger, but not heavier, and hold well.

In selecting an anchor for a boat, you should consult the tables that recommend anchors for different sizes and types of boats. These can be found in standard nautical reference books, such as Chapman's *Piloting,* or in booklets from anchor manufacturers.

In general, the type of anchor popular in your section of the country is a good one to consider first. Experienced boatmen know what holds best in their cruising grounds.

The rode. There are several ways that the anchor line, or *rode,* can be attached to the anchor. If your anchor is not permanently made up, you can attach the line quickly with an anchor bend (see page 107). Usually there is an eyesplice, with thimble, already made up on the end of the line with a shackle that is attached to the anchor. Careful seamen wire the anchor shackle so that it can't work loose. A long-lasting setup would be a combination of shackle, a short length of anchor chain, and another shackle to the anchor line.

On small boats the anchor and line are set up all the time. On larger boats the most-used anchor and chain are chocked on deck, and the line is stowed below and brought on deck when needed. Nylon rope is generally used for anchor line because its elasticity makes the boat ride more comfortably without the sudden surges that can work the anchor out.

Weighing anchor. To get the anchor up, or to weigh anchor, under power, the helmsman steers very slowly toward the anchor as the crew hauls in the slack line, until the boat is directly over the anchor. Normally, an upward pull on the line will break the anchor loose from the bottom. But, if the wind has blown hard all night, the anchor may have dug itself so deep that arm power won't be enough to break it out. In this case, the skipper will first try the standard method of freeing an anchor: by

These anchors are among the more common designs. The best anchor to choose is usually the one that is most popular in your cruising area.

Most large boats have two, the second with added weight for storms or a different shape for different bottom conditions.

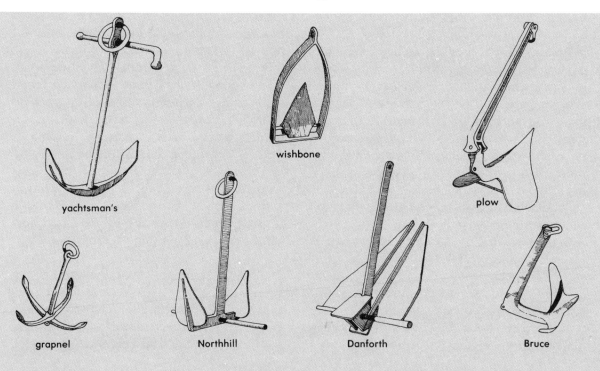

yachtsman's

wishbone

plow

grapnel

Northhill

Danforth

Bruce

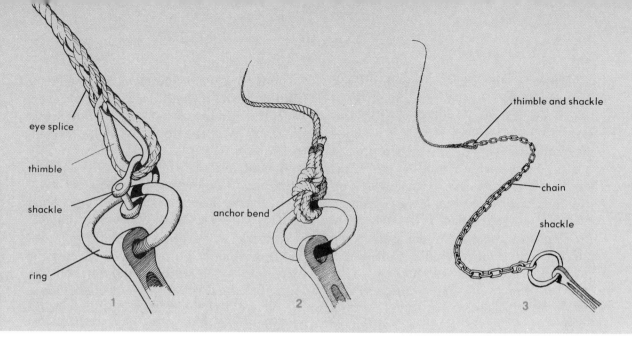

eye splice

thimble

shackle

ring

anchor bend

thimble and shackle

chain

shackle

1   2   3

Three ways to attach the anchor rode to the anchor are shown. An eye splice over a thimble, plus a shackle (1) is good if you are anchoring briefly, or making up a second anchor. An anchor bend (2) is used on a small boat that anchors infrequently. A short length of chain between rode and anchor (3) is usually the best method for cruising boats.

using power and moving straight ahead or by sailing out, he can usually pull the anchor free from the mud or clay suction that is holding it.

Sometimes another solution is needed, however. One alternative is to send the crew forward to put the bow down, and then make the anchor line fast. The crew then moves aft all at once, to make the bow rise and, with luck, break the anchor free.

As the anchor comes up to the surface, the person handling it tries to slosh off the mud; jerking the anchor up or down a few times in the water will usually wash it clean. Sometimes a few buckets of water and a few passes with a mop (properly called a *swab*) may be necessary. Then the anchor is secured in its chocks, and the rode is carefully coiled down and stowed. The rode will be easier to handle next time you need it if you tie the coil in several places with lengths of light line to keep it neat.

Here are two other situations that call for anchoring. If your boat is becalmed, doesn't have a motor, and the current is moving it toward rocks, speedy anchoring is the solution. Or you might want to stop somewhere for lunch or to fish. In such a case, a short scope will probably hold, but you had better keep watch to make sure that you're not dragging into an area you want to avoid—a busily traveled channel.

Sometimes—when nosing a boat up to a beach, for example—it's useful to put out a stern anchor (see page 81).

Mooring. A mooring anchor is extremely heavy, shaped like a mushroom, and set on the bottom for the season or longer. Once dug in, the anchor's shape and weight keep it in place; a chain adds weight and strength, and a very strong rope pendant goes from the top of the chain to the mooring buoy, which marks the spot. Usually there is relatively little scope on permanent moorings, but always enough for the highest tide that can be expected.

Picking up a mooring under power is a relatively simple boat-handling situation. First observe boats moored nearby for information about the wind and current. Then approach the mooring buoy, moving in the direction in which the moored sailboats are pointing. (Moored mo-

Good boat handling involves good steering technique. Now and then look back to check your wake; practice steering until the wake is straight, and you'll find you make better time.

torboats may lie somewhat differently from sailboats if there is a current running. With their high cabins and shallow keels they may be more affected by the wind than by the current.)

Slow up, and do your level best to come to a complete stop just as you reach the buoy. (Use reverse if necessary.) Your crew then reaches for the pickup, and you're home.

Mooring under power is easier than mooring without power. Simply drop your sails out in the harbor, and rely on the motor for steady control of the boat. This is a good way to learn mooring procedure, especially if you have a new boat.

Picking up a mooring under sail, like anchoring, requires more skill. When you do it well, under the scrutiny of people watching from other boats, you are entitled to feel a certain pride. All it takes is knowledge of the basic method and a sense of timing.

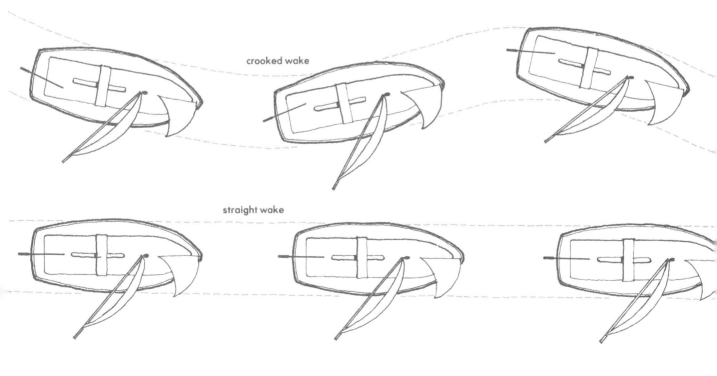

crooked wake

straight wake

The best method is to shorten sail so that you are down to the smallest sail setup that gives you full steerage way. You then approach the mooring from the most convenient direction, intending to round up and be heading into the wind perhaps two boat lengths away from the buoy. On a small boat like the D-C it might be only one boat length. It depends on the wind conditions, too. If your timing is right, you come to a stop with the bow right at the buoy, and before you start to drift away, your crew picks up the buoy, brings it and the end of the pendant aboard, and makes the pendant fast.

If the situation is complicated by a current as well as wind, you may have to round up somewhat differently. No problem. Just point your boat in the same direction the moored sailboats are heading, and make sure your sheets are loose so the sails are luffing. You can coast against the current just as well as against the wind.

Getting away from a mooring under sail is usually not a problem either, if done with care. Often one side will be better to go off on because of nearby boats. Get the sails up, and trimmed moderately, while still keeping fast to the buoy. The boat will alternately tack first one way and then the other, not going more than a few feet. Time your move so that you cast off the mooring buoy when you're moving on the tack you want to be on.

Another way to get off a mooring is to have the crew back the jib on the side opposite the one you want to go off on; once the bow has been pushed in the desired direction, let the jib go, drop the mooring buoy, and trim both sails.

Some fine points of steering. Steering a

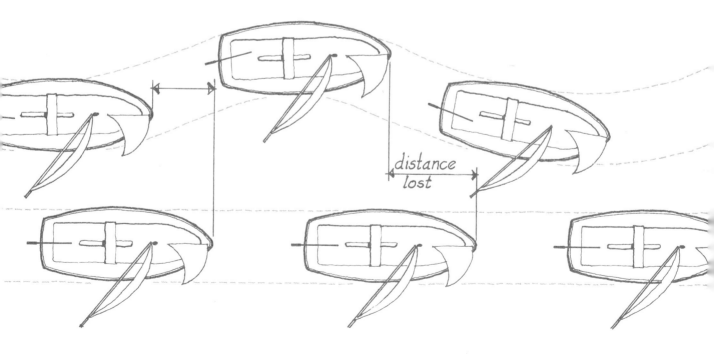

distance lost

sailboat is an art. The first thing to remember is that a sailboat will steer only when water is moving past the rudder. Because the wind and waves can be misleading, beginners must learn to sense when a boat is moving through the water and when it is stalled or standing still. You need this sense, especially in tricky sailing situations—such as getting in irons and getting out—but you also need it when approaching a mooring. The slower you go, the less steering control you have, so don't

Getting away from a dock in a crowded harbor is sometimes easier with just one sail, usually the main. When you're clear of other boats you can get the other sail up.

expect to make significant changes in direction at the last minute.

Steering properly means steering in a straight line. Compared to steering a wheeled vehicle this requires attentiveness, very small adjustments, and a fingertip sense that comes only with practice. It is easy to oversteer any boat or ship, and it takes a special knack when waves are constantly moving the boat. Steering in a straight line means accuracy in getting where you intend to go; in a race, this can be equated with speed.

The simple way of steering a straight

course is to sight on a fixed object far away—a buoy, smokestack, or church steeple—and keep it directly ahead of you.

Another way of steering is by the compass. The beginner is often surprised to find when steering by a compass that the boat seems to go the wrong way when he moves the tiller or wheel. This is because his eyes have been looking at the wrong part of the compass; in a way he's seeing an illusion. The compass card doesn't turn. It floats free in the compass and remains more or less stationary; the boat turns around the card. The *lubber line,* the thin white post at the front of the compass, moves with the boat. So if you are steering a course of 28 degrees and the compass card seems to move to the left, it's really the boat that's moved to the right—the lubber line has moved with it and is now pointing at 35 degrees. To get back on course, think: "I am steering the lubber line toward the 28-degree mark on the card." It's a bit confusing at first, but it gets easier with practice. (See the drawing.)

A good way to check your steering is to look at the boat's wake—a crooked wake is a bad sign. If you're sailing in rough water though, it is often impossible to keep the boat from swinging back and forth.

A third way to steer is by the wind. This is the hardest to do consistently, because it requires a fine touch on the helm and a keen feel for the wind; practice on a day when the wind is steady. This technique is important when you're sailing close-hauled, because you are trying to keep moving upwind as much as possible. The trick is to keep watching your telltales, so that when the wind and their angle change, you change

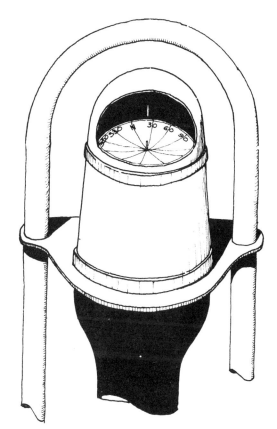

Steering by compass takes practice. Watch the lubber line, here indicating 28 degrees on the compass card; steer the boat so the lubber line moves toward your course. Don't try to "steer the card"; it is not moving—it just seems to be.

course, too, keeping the sails full, but on the edge of luffing.

One more thing to remember about steering is that *it is the stern of the boat that turns.* Those used to front-wheel steering in a car must adjust to this difference when steering a boat. It doesn't matter much when you are coming about in open water, but when you steer up to or away from a dock, or turn close to another boat, watch your stern.

MOORING UNDER SAIL

When mooring under sail, head into the wind, after allowing the right amount of space to coast up to the buoy.

If your timing is right, your crew can pick up the mooring buoy just as the boat coasts to a halt. You may have to try again.

So far, we've concentrated on sailing and handling your own boat, without regard to other boats on the water. You'll be meeting other boats soon enough, however, so let's take a moment to outline the rules that tell boats how to avoid collisions. The Rules of the Road, as they're officially called, are long and complicated. Someday you should study such matters as the navigation lights boats carry at night, how the kind of boat you're in affects your movements, how the kind of boat you're crossing, meeting, or passing affects your own movements, and a great many other considerations.

For now, let's concentrate on two basic groups of rules that are easy to learn and essential to safe sailing.

Right of way. When two **sailboats** meet, the following rules should be kept in mind:

▲ The boat on the starboard tack has the right of way over the boat on the port tack.
▲ If both boats have the wind on the same side, that is, if they are sailing on the same tack, the boat that is to windward must keep out of the way of the boat that is to leeward.
▲ A boat running free (downwind) must keep clear of a boat that is close-hauled.

Boats under power. It is not always true that a sailboat has the right of way over a boat under power. The exceptions are important:

▲ A sailboat overtaking a powerboat, like any boat overtaking another, does *not* have the right of way.

A sailboat normally has the right of way over a powerboat, but not always. Don't let a spin- *naker or a jib keep you from watching ahead at all times.*

▲ A power-driven vessel restricted in its ability to maneuver—as in a narrow channel, when fishing, or handling navigational buoys—has the right of way over a sailboat.

▲ A sailboat, like any other vessel, should keep a lookout and be ready to avoid collision and sound a warning if collision is imminent.

▲ A sailboat using its motor, even with the sails up, is considered to be under power, and must follow the right-of-way rules for powered vessels.

DOCKING

Bringing a boat in to a dock is a special situation. Come in slowly, while maintaining steerage way. Under most circumstances, you dock with the bow of the boat headed into the wind or current (whichever is stronger), because this gives you both braking effect and, if there is a current, additional steerage control. You dock, when possible, with an eye to the way you will leave the dock.

If there is a choice, take the leeward side of the dock. This way the wind will be blowing the boat away from the dock, which minimizes wear and tear on the boat and also makes it easier to leave the dock.

Docking lines. Proper docking means putting out proper dock lines, not only to secure the boat while it is tied up, but to help get away from the dock. Because there are slips, finger piers, floating docks, and variations that include mooring to pilings, tying up is a subject that could fill a small book. On this page is a gull's eye view of a typical dock.

A small dinghy can be tied up, generally speaking, by only its *painter* or tow line. Even so, the stern might also be tied to keep the boat from getting in someone else's way. If you bring a small sailboat in

Proper use of dock lines varies with the size of the boat and the length of time it will be docked. Two lines, one at bow and one at stern, will do for a brief stop (1). If the wind or current is strong, use a forward spring line (2). For an extended stay, use fenders, fender boards, and two spring lines (3). A dinghy or small boat can also be tied in a slip (4).

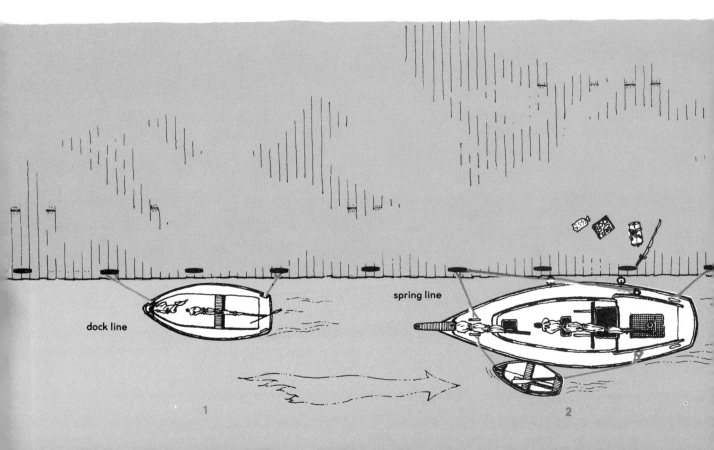

dock line

spring line

1

2

to a dock for a brief stop, and someone stays with the boat, a bow line and a stern line will usually suffice. If there is a current or much wind from ahead, an additional line is run from the stern to a cleat on the dock approximately even with the bow. This line, called a *spring line,* keeps the boat from moving backward and lets the shorter bow and stern lines hold the boat at a proper distance from the dock. One spring line is shown on the center boat at the dock in the drawing. However, this would be sufficient for only a short time and only if the boat is attended. Sooner or later the current or wind will change, and then good docking practice requires a second spring line from the bow aft.

The other function of the spring lines is to help you get away from the dock, especially if the wind is against you. There are a number of ways to use spring lines: to turn a boat, to warp them around the corner of a dock, to get away when there are other boats close by, and others. To study these, you should refer to a comprehensive book on seamanship.

In the drawing on page 115, besides the four dock lines on the largest boat, you will also see a pair of fenders and a fender board. Always hang these out when tying up, to keep the boat well away from any rough pilings or dock edges.

A last point of interest: both a sailboat under power and a destroyer are often *backed* away from a dock because that's the easiest way to get off.

fender board

3

4

8

WIND AND WATER

Wind is invisible. You can feel it, you can often smell it, and you can see what it does. You can also forecast it, if not very precisely. And you can acquire an understanding of the wind and how it affects the water, particularly, how it affects your boat and its sails. But the first thing you have to learn about the sailor's wind is its direction. *Always be aware of the direction from which the wind is blowing.*

This photograph of an Atlantic ghosting without enough wind to disturb a smoke ring is a scene of quiet frustration. In such circumstances, keep watch for any sign of a breeze, such as a dark patch on the water, to head for.

One of the conventions concerning the wind is that it is named by the direction it blows from, not the direction it blows toward. A north wind comes from the north, a sou'wester blows out of the southwest. It's important to remember this distinction, because, unlike the wind, a boat's course is described by the direction in which it is going, and so are the currents in the water—a southerly current is moving to the south.

A knowledgeable sailor is aware of the direction and force of the wind long before he reaches the dock. The wind determines which way he'll leave the dock or mooring, what sails he'll set, and whether he'll need

BEAUFORT NO.		M.P.H	KNOTS	WIND DESCRIPTION	EFFECT OF WIND ON SEA
Force	0	Less than 1		Calm	Sea smooth and glassy
Force	1	1-3	1-3	Light air	Ripples; surface is ruffled by wind; some smooth patches may remain
Force	2	4-7	4-6	Light breeze	Entire suface ruffled; small wavelets short, but pronounced; crests glassy
Force	3	8-12	7-10	Gentle breeze	Large wavelets; occasional whitecaps
Force	4	13-18	11-16	Moderate breeze	Small waves, becoming longer; about half the waves show whitecaps
Force	5	19-24	17-21	Fresh breeze	Moderate waves of a pronounced long form; most crests show whitecaps; some spray
Force	6	25-31	22-27	Strong breeze	Large waves begin to form; whitecaps everywhere; foam and spray
Force	7	32-38	28-33	Moderate gale	Sea heaps up; white foam from crests blows in streaks
Force	8	39-46	34-40	Fresh gale	Moderately high waves; edges of crests spume; heavier streaks of foam
Force	9	47-54	41-47	Strong gale	High waves; dense streaks of foam; spray may affect visibility
Force	10	55-63	48-55	Whole gale	Very high waves with long overhanging crests; great foam patches; much spray
Force	11	64-72	56-63	Storm	Exceptionally high waves; foam patches cover sea; wave crests blown into froth
Force	12	73+	64+	Hurricane (Atlantic) Typhoon (Pacific)	Air filled with foam and spray; sea completely white with driving spray

WATER SCALE

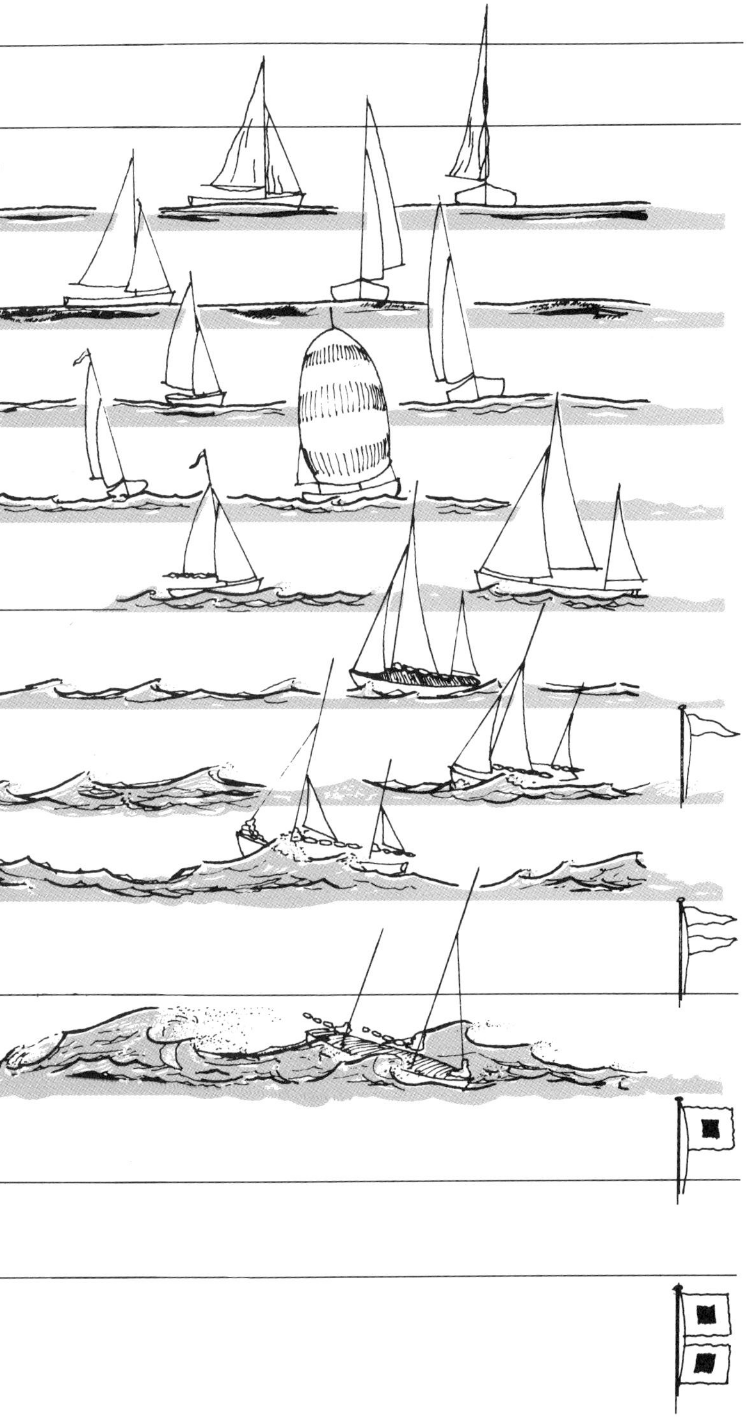

EFFECT OF WIND ON BOATS 15 TO 40 FT.

Becalmed; no steerageway; sails slat

Sufficient way on for steering; sails take airfoil shape loosely

Boats sail easily and begin to heel

Good sailing

Small boats shorten sail; large ones carry working sails, Genoas

Small boats, reefed mainsail only; large boats shorten sail

Small boats return to port; larger craft double reef

Storm canvas

Bare poles; lie ahull or run off with great care

Lie to sea anchor or run off, streaming drogue

Lie to sea anchor

Seek shelter if possible

Seek shelter if possible

Blowing smoke is one good way to watch for a fitful breeze.

warm clothes. So, how do you keep track of the wind's direction?

If you're still ashore, look for a flag; watch for cigarette smoke or the plume of smoke from a stack or chimney. Look for the way boats are lying relative to their moorings—generally they will weathervane, that is, swing around and point into the wind. (Be careful though: in light air a boat is more likely to swing to a strong current.)

If you're aboard the boat, look first for the telltales tied to shrouds and stays. Many boats also have a pennant, fly, or weathervane at the top of the mast that indicates wind direction. Some boats have electronic instruments that read out wind direction and wind strength on dials.

You can also learn to judge the wind by the water's surface. On a normal day the waves seem to move across the water in the same direction as the wind, but in light air it is often hard to tell which way the wavelets are going. When all other aids fail, you have to learn to feel the wind on your neck and face. This is the sailor's ultimate wind gauge.

Apparent wind. When you get underway, you'll discover subtle but important changes in the wind's direction and strength. As the boat moves through the water, the wind on your cheek and in the sails is called the *apparent wind,* which is not the same as the true wind you felt while standing on the dock. The boat's forward movement creates its own wind, which combines with the true wind to produce a wind different in direction and strength. This apparent wind is a complicated effect that depends on the speed of the boat, the strength and direction of the true wind, and the point of sailing you're on. For example: if you're sailing on a reach at right angles to the true wind, the apparent wind comes from farther forward. Or, to put it another way, the wind direction shown by your telltale is ahead of the true wind. If you are sailing close-hauled, the boat's speed adds to the speed of the true wind, making the apparent wind stronger. Sailing downwind, the boat's speed subtracts from the true wind, making the apparent wind weaker; this is not an illusion—the wind the boat is sailing in really is less strong.

Wind strength. Besides the wind's direction, you need to know its strength. The well-known Beaufort wind scale was devised by a nineteenth-century British rear admiral named Francis Beaufort; he measured the wind's force not by miles per hour, but by the effect of different strengths of wind on the water relative to the sailing vessels of his day. In the scale provided in this chapter we have adapted Beaufort's definitions to modern craft; thus, instead of saying "fishing smacks take in two reefs," we show a cruising yawl under jib and mizzen.

Beaufort identified the different wind strengths by the word "force" plus a number: you will hear some sailors describing a wind as "force 4" or "force 6." After a while, you'll get a sense of how strong a wind force 6 is, without translating it into nautical miles per hour. However, most marine weather reports, including those of the National Weather Service, do use knots, and this is what most people recognize.

Another thing to know about the wind is that it's usually stronger the higher up it blows, not only way up, at 30,000 feet, but twenty or forty feet up. That means it may be blowing harder at your masthead than it is on deck, which explains why a sixty-foot yawl may glide quietly past when your nimble little boat seems to be becalmed.

Thus, wind strength also affects reefing. When you reef, or if you switch to a smaller jib on a large boat, you not only reduce the sail area at the bottom, but you actually make a more important reduction at the top where the wind has more leverage.

Wind forecasting. You can learn something about forecasting the wind without taking up the whole science of meteorology. In many local situations you can learn by listening to other sailors and by watching the daily rhythms of the wind. Summer winds in many localities tend to spring up in midafternoon, usually from a predictable direction. Each lake, bay, or other general area may vary, depending on how the sun warms a nearby land mass or how the larger ocean winds work with or against the local breezes.

Sources of weather information that help you know what the wind is going to do are readily available. The daily weather map published in many city newspapers is a valuable tool. If you are planning a sailing cruise, clip the weather maps for four or five days ahead; the pattern of weather moving across the country is then easy to spot. In North America, for instance, weather systems tend to move from west to east, at a rate of about 300 miles a day in summer and 400 miles a day in winter.

Once you get used to weather maps and learn to find out where the day's low-pressure area is, remember the following: in the northern hemisphere, when you face the wind, the low-pressure area will always be on your right. Low pressure often indicates clouds, rain, and wind are coming.

Following are several ways in which water and the atmosphere act upon each other.

1. Fog is the result of the interaction between air and water of different temperatures.

2. The change of tide often brings a wind.

3. A long continued wind will build up waves and eventually create a current; con-

Rain tends to flatten waves.

versely, it can slow a current that would otherwise be faster.

Electronic wind instruments that show the direction and force of apparent wind are often carried on large cruising and racing boats. Similar instruments can be mounted in your home if you like to keep watch on the wind's vagaries.

For a small boat, the instrumentation to use is telltales. They can be simple pieces of yarn (see page 58) or any of the commercial variations that are available. In addition, a small cruising boat should have a barometer aboard, and also a radio, which is one of the most useful weather devices there is. A radio will bring you not only weather forecasts and normal reports on weather conditions, but two other kinds of useful information as well: calamity warnings and static.

Twenty minutes before one well-remembered Fourth of July squall hit Long Island Sound, high winds disrupted a ball game at Yankee Stadium. Sailors listening

The angry sea in the distance may be breaking over a sandbar; keep clear of water like this.

on their radios had ample warning of trouble; the smart ones took precautions and saved themselves from capsizing. The other squall sign often heard on portable radios is static, which gets loud and crackly just before a lightning storm bursts upon the scene.

Squalls. Squalls call for special caution on the water, because the wind can reach gale force for a few minutes. Unless you are very experienced and sailing in a rugged boat, be very leery of squalls. Learn to see and feel them coming. An afternoon build-up of clouds, especially an anvil-shaped thunder cloud, is the most obvious signal. Constant observation in your normal cruising area soon teaches you which squalls are coming toward you and which are going away. When your sailing wind drops to zero, the skies turn dark, and you feel a heaviness in the air, watch out. Get your foul-weather gear handy, stow the items that might be damaged by rain or blow overboard, and shorten sail. Most small boats, if they have plenty of sea room, can easily ride out even a fierce squall with all sails taken in. If the wind is too overpowering, and you don't mind some fast work, try dropping the jib or the main and sailing on just one sail until the squall is over.

Squalls are a law unto themselves, and their behavior is unpredictable; but there is one thing to remember, in general, about long-lasting storms that is fairly dependable in most areas of the United States: weather from the east is usually bad. Watch out when the forecast is "easterly winds."

Old sailors usually have a store of axioms about the wind—some of them can be helpful in predicting the weather, but take them with a grain of salt.

Finding the wind. Use your powers of observation when looking for the wind. If you're almost becalmed—just ghosting along—and you see dark streaks on the water, head for them and you'll pick up the wind sooner. If you watch other boats, you'll often see them start to heel and move ten minutes before you feel the freshening breeze. Head for the action.

A few words about the wind. Following are a few nautical terms that describe the wind.

If the wind is gusty and gradually changing direction, as it often is, there are two ways it could be shifting. If the change is in a clockwise direction, the wind is said to be *veering,* or *hauling.* If the gradual change is counterclockwise, the wind is *backing.*

If the wind increases steadily in strength,

it is *freshening;* momentary increases are *puffs.*

If the wind changes direction so that it is more nearly ahead of you when you are close reaching or sailing close-hauled, then you are being *headed,* whether or not the wind is backing or veering at the time. If the wind shift is the other way, thus making it easier to get where you're going without having to tack, then you have gotten a *lift.*

Waves and water. Wind makes waves (though the shape of the sea bottom and the action of currents also have their effects on waves), and when sailing, you have to deal with them constantly. The first thing to know is that not only are you more comfortable in smooth water, but your boat goes faster. Therefore it is worth finding the smoothest waters you can. Sometimes you have no choice. If you want to go from one place to another, the water is rough, and there's no alternate route, you have to take the waves and the spray. But at other times, you can choose to sail on the side of the bay where the sea has not built up, or you may be able to take the route close to the windward shore, or behind an island. Or, if you know that high winds are forecast, you can start earlier or plan your day's outing to suit the weather. Making such wise choices is good seamanship.

When the wind has a long fetch across the water, waves build up. But when a point of land or an island makes a lee, you can find smoother water there, at least for part of a trip.

In each case, the behavior of local waters is something you have to figure out for

On a sultry afternoon, as thunderclouds build up, a small boat's crew should be ready to drop sails if a squall hits and perhaps ride out the blow under the jib.

yourself. In one place a long sandbar may help kick up short, choppy waves, because of the way a shallow bottom affects the moving water. In another case, a tidal current may help you sail quicker. Instead of bucking a current for four hours, start earlier or later and you'll sometimes save half a day.

Weather has been talked and written about for centuries. Some of the books that help you understand it make good additions to an advanced sailor's library.

To fasten a flag staff to an endless flag halyard, make three half hitches (a clove hitch plus an extra half hitch) for both upper and lower ends of the staff. Slip the staff through one set of hitches at a time, adjust and tighten them, hoist the staff, and the burgee will fly securely in an upright position.

9

SAILORS' SKILLS

Of all the skills you need to be competent on a modern sailboat, none hark back more directly to the old windjammer days than the handy skills of marlinespike seamanship: knots, hitches, bends, splicing, whipping, and general line handling. You certainly don't have to know all the exotic tricks of this ancient trade, but a basic knowledge is essential. In the following pages you will find a primer of marlinespike seamanship.

ROPE

The sailor's skills we're discussing start with a knowledge of rope. Manila rope, in the old days, came in coils, and it was nec-essary to take the new rope from the inside of the coil, so it wouldn't kink. Today's synthetic ropes come on spools and are far better than manila. Most of them are stronger, size for size. They are easier to handle and they don't rot. The knots, bends, and hitches are the same, but there are some small differences in the ways you tie them, chiefly because synthetic rope tends to be a little more slippery than manila. For example, a nylon or Dacron splice should be a little longer than a manila or hemp rope splice.

The three main types of synthetic material used for rope are easy to distinguish by look, feel, and weight. *Nylon* has the

ROPE: HOW IT'S MADE AND HOW IT'S COILED

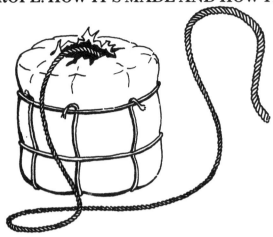

Rope used to come in coils, and it would be drawn out from the inside; today it's wrapped around rollers.

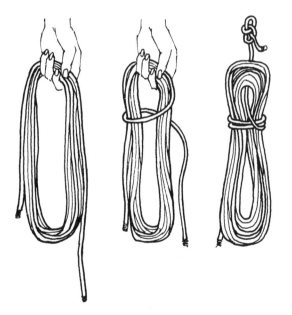

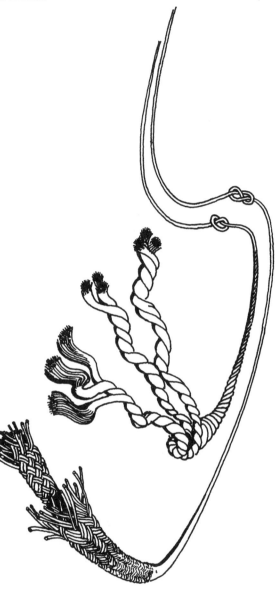

Coil line clockwise, then take a turn or two around the coils with your free hand, slip the end over the turns and through the coils, tie it with two half hitches and hang the coils on a cleat.

Three-strand and braided line (one braid inside the other) are the most common types of rope. The figure-eight knot (top) is a good "stopper"; the overhand knot is not.

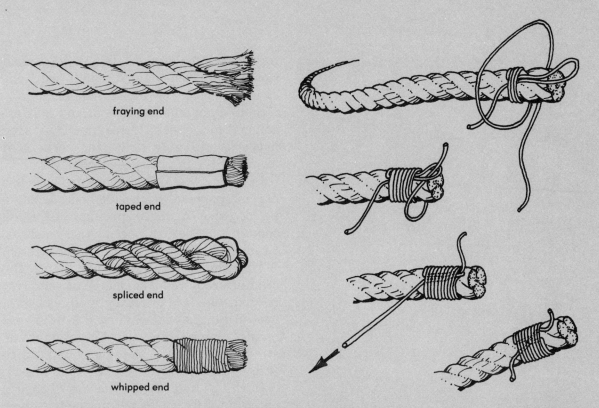

The end of laid rope must be secured to keep it from fraying. For a brief fix, taping will do, but for a permanent solution either splice or whip the end. If the line will run through blocks, whip it to avoid making the line too thick.

Moving from top to bottom, plain whipping is wound around a long loop laid along the line. The free end of the whipping is then inserted through the loop and pulled under the turns to secure both ends. The ends are then trimmed.

most stretch; this is desirable in anchor lines and dock lines, which need some give. *Dacron* or Terrylene (Dacron's British equivalent) has the least elasticity, and for that reason is best for halyards, sheets, vangs, and guys. And *polypropylene* is the lightest; it actually floats, which makes it good for dinghy painters—no one needs a dinghy painter caught in the propeller. But polypropylene isn't very strong, and it deteriorates rapidly in sunlight. When used for towing a dinghy, polypropylene rope should be large in diameter.

Rope, or line as it's called when it's working on a ship or boat, is made in several ways. The most familiar variety is three-strand laid rope. Each strand is made by laying, or twisting, many smaller strands together; then, the three resulting strands are twisted in the opposite direction to make the final rope. For centuries, most rope has been made this way, and virtually all rope made today is twisted in this manner. It's called "right-handed"

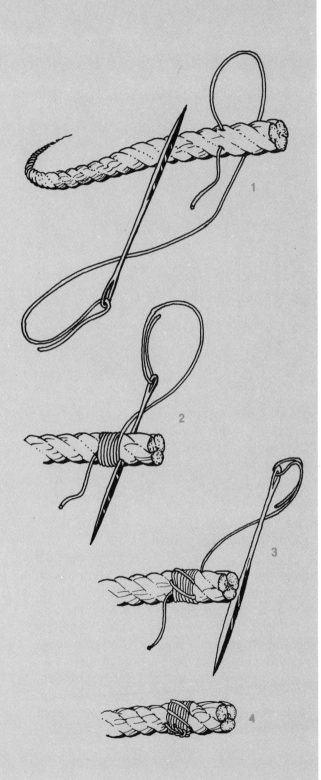

rope, and it should always be coiled clockwise. Occasionally, you'll see four-strand rope, and even "left-handed" rope.

Some light line is braided, and it is excellent for special uses such as flag halyards or tying down the corners of awnings. It can't be spliced, however.

In recent years, double-braided rope has become popular. Its braided core inside a braided sheath makes splicing possible, although you need a special tool to do it. Braided Dacron rope has minimum stretch.

The choice of line depends on the strength required, the degree of elasticity needed, the ease of slicing, and, at times, special qualities such as how it feels in your hands. A small-diameter jibsheet might be strong enough, for example, but hard to hold or pull. A bigger size is easier to use.

In the United States, the size of rope is determined by its diameter, which is given in inches and fractions thereof. In Great Britain, rope size is determined by the circumference.

Coiling. The first thing you need to know about line is how to coil it. When not in use, all lines should be coiled for stowage. Don't

---

Sailmaker's whipping is sturdier and looks neater than any other. It requires a needle and waxed string. Make a stitch through the rope to secure it, then wrap the string as for plain whipping, pulling each turn taut (1). Make another stitch through the rope, bringing the needle out as close as possible to the last turn (2). Make a diagonal overcast stitch along the edge of each strand of the rope, stitching over the whipping and through the rope each time, as shown, to secure the turns (3). When done, (4) finish by trimming loose ends of string and rope.

try to coil a line around your elbow, the way your Aunt Tilly used to coil clothesline. The coils will be too small, they won't hang properly, and they'll tangle.

There's a better way. First, make sure the line is free and not kinked or knotted. Overhaul it, if necessary, just to make sure it's completely free running. Second, hold the end of the line and the coils in your left hand, and make each coil clockwise with your right hand. At first you may find the coils vary in size, but you'll soon learn how to swing your right arm the same distance for each coil to make them even.

Third, make sure the coils turn clockwise, and try to lay each coil next to, instead of on top of, the previous one in your hand. If you turn the rope the wrong way, the line will become unruly and if you overlap the coils they'll tangle when the line is uncoiled. As you coil the line, give it a small twist with your wrist now and then to keep the coils hanging right.

The drawings on page 128 show how to make up a coil for stowage. If you've just hoisted a sail and are coiling the halyard, the coil should be hung on the cleat, ready to be let go in a hurry.

Rope ends. If you leave the cut ends of a piece of rope the way you buy it, the ends will fray, untwist, or unbraid, ending up a

---

The tree climber's back splice is little known in boating, but it is very useful for any sheet that must go through a block because it is not bulky. To make it, follow the instructions at right, keeping in mind that rope is generally made of three strands, each of which is in turn made of three strands.

Separate one end of a piece of rope into three strands, then separate each of the three strands in two, leaving one single strand (a, b, and c) and two interwound strands that will be cut away when the splice is completed (1). Once by one, insert each individual strand under the single strand next to it, moving counterclockwise (2). Pull the strands tight (3). Weave each of the single strands in and out of the rope as shown to bury the end; then trim the remaining loose strands ½" (13 mm) from the splice (4).

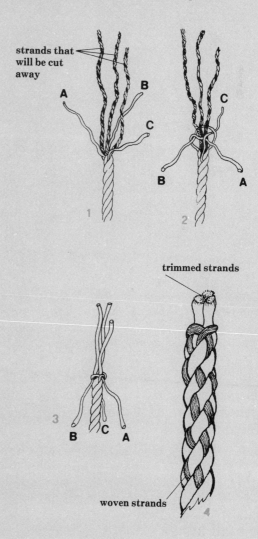

strands that will be cut away

A   B

C

B   A

1

C

2

trimmed strands

3

B C A

woven strands

4

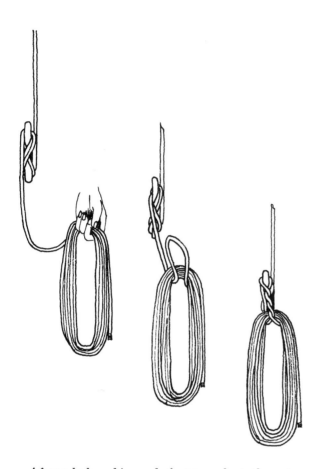

After a halyard is made fast to a cleat, the extra line is coiled as shown here, then hung on the cleat so it will be ready to run when the sail is dropped. Keep all halyards free of tangle.

trical tape or rigging tape will last awhile), or melt the ends over a match, a candle, or a stove burner, if the rope is synthetic. Melting the ends isn't permanent either, but it's a quick and easy way to keep the line from unraveling. Be careful: The melted fibers stay hot longer than you think; don't touch them with bare fingers until the fibers have cooled. You'll get a neater finish if you smooth the melted strands with a cloth while they're soft.

Whipping. To finish a rope end so that it will stay firm and tight enough to reeve through a block, *whip it.* This is done with marline or sailmaker's twine, and a standard whipping that will do for most purposes can be made in a few minutes (see drawings, page 129). A better method of whipping, which requires a needle and a sailmaker's palm to push the needle, is called a sailmaker's whipping (see drawing, page 130).

End splices. Another way to finish the end of a rope is to make a splice at the end. The standard back splice is long lasting, but it enlarges the end of the line and can't be used if the line must be frequently rove through a block or fairlead. The tree climber's back splice (shown on page 131) is a much better choice for such use, since it doesn't enlarge the end of a line.

Dock lines are convenient to use if you make an eye splice in one or both ends. The eye splice is the easiest splice to learn and can be done in a few minutes. Here again, with synthetic lines, a little melting is a good way to take care of the last semi-frayed ends.

nuisance. But what you do to a rope end depends on how you'll use it.

If you need a spare line, you should protect the ends until you make up a dock line or sheet. There are two simple solutions to this. Either tape the end, if the rope is made of natural or synthetic fiber (elec-

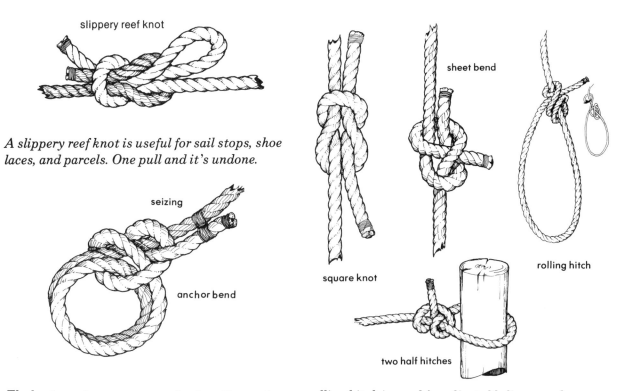

slippery reef knot

A slippery reef knot is useful for sail stops, shoe laces, and parcels. One pull and it's undone.

seizing

anchor bend

sheet bend

square knot

rolling hitch

two half hitches

The best way to secure an anchor bend is to seize the end to the standing part (top). The square knot is overrated; it's good for tying a furled sail, but should not be used for joining lines; the

rolling hitch is good for adjustable lines, such as those on awnings or fenders; a sheet bend is a good way to tie two lines together; and two half hitches has a hundred uses.

KNOTS

Of the thousands of knots seamen have devised, only a few are necessary for the modern small-boat sailor to learn. The diagrams in this chapter show the basic ones.

Follow the drawings carefully, and practice each knot until you can tie it without stopping to figure out the next move. Tie the knot forward, backward, and upside down; otherwise you'll be stumped some day when you have to tie a knot in a hurry with the free end coming in differently from the way you first learned it.

All really useful knots have three important qualities: (1) they are easy to tie; (2) they will always hold if tied properly; and (3) they are easy to untie even after they've taken a heavy strain. If you are ever tempted to secure something on a boat with a lash-up that doesn't satisfy these three requirements, don't. It will only get you in trouble.

The simplest knot of all is the *overhand knot* (see page 128), but since it is hard to untie after being pulled tight, it isn't good for much. If you make one more loop before putting the end through, however, it becomes a *figure-eight knot,* which will untie. This serves as a stopper knot at the end of a line that keeps the line from pulling through a block.

The *square knot,* or reef knot (page 133), is an old favorite that everyone learns; but it, too, has a tendency to jam under strain. Use it only when doing a job you won't have to undo in a hurry. Never use a square knot to tie two lines together. A better way to tie reef points or sail stops is to use a reef knot without pulling one end through (page 133); this is sometimes called a *slippery hitch.* One pull on the bow end, and the knot comes undone.

Many sailors feel that the *bowline* (page 135) is the most useful knot used on a boat. Once you learn it, you can tie it in three seconds; it makes a loop as large or small as you need; it holds forever; and it can always be untied. Some call it the "king of knots."

Less regal but decidedly useful is the *rolling hitch* (page 133). Use it when you don't want a line to slide along a spar, wire, or other line you are tying it to. When loose, the knot will slip; when strained, it holds. This makes the knot particularly handy when you need to adjust the length or tension of a line, as on a deck awning, for example.

Two *half hitches* (page 133) is a knot that's easy to learn and useful for tying a line to a stanchion or a ring bolt. An excellent variation is called the *anchor bend* (page 133). The anchor bend was traditionally used to tie the line to an anchor. It has been largely supplanted in that job by the shackle, but it is still useful for tying a line to something, such as a bucket, when the simple loop of the bowline won't do.

A variation on two half hitches is the *clove hitch* (page 135), which is widely used for tying a dinghy's painter or a docking line to a piling or a bollard, or for tying fenders to the lifelines of larger boats. For this job the clove hitch has the advantage of being adjustable without having to be untied if you need to shorten or lengthen the line. If you're using slippery line or are tying up to a large piling, secure the clove hitch by making two more half hitches with the end, around the standing part. In general, the clove hitch has limitations and should be used sparingly.

A special adaptation of the clove hitch is shown at the beginning of this chapter; it is used to fasten a flag halyard to a flagstaff that is to be hoisted to the masthead. Here you have no free end to work with, so while you're trying to fasten the flagstaff, the halyard won't break loose from your fingers and fly off in the wind, and it won't come tumbling down. The illustration shows how to make and tighten the hitches, hoist the flag, and make the halyard fast. The staff will be held tight and vertical, with the burgee flying free in the wind above the halyard block and the masthead. This is a good use of the clove hitch and a half.

DOCK LINES

You are a willing but inexperienced guest helping as a boat comes in to a dock: you leap ashore, dock line in hand, and begin to pull at the line. You're wrong! Unless the skipper directs otherwise, you should get ashore and just hold the dock line, to keep the boat steady until a stern line can be

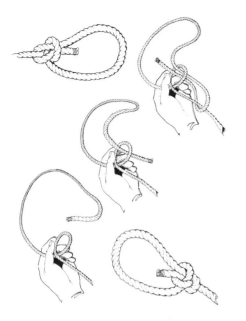

The bowline is undoubtedly the most useful knot a sailor can learn. It makes a quick loop, won't slip, and can always be untied.

made fast. If it's necessary to pull the boat a few feet farther up the dock, do it slowly. Yanking on a dock line fastened to the bow of a boat usually makes the boat pivot so that the bow swings in and the stern goes out. This only makes it harder to take care of the stern line. When the boat is in proper position, make the bow line fast. Then go aft and help with the stern line. Probably both lines will need to be adjusted, and spring lines added to keep the boat securely in place (see Chapter 7).

To hold or secure a line aboard a boat or on the dock, cleat the line under most circumstances to make it fast. The drawings on page 136 show the correct method for cleating a line: take one turn around the bottom of the cleat first, then wrap the line in a couple of figure eights around the cleat. Two or three figure eights will make the line hold, four or five are lubberly. To avoid the problem of knocking off a turn accidentally, make the last turn with the free end of the line looped under itself, and pull the line taut. This makes another kind of half hitch that will hold. Don't do this with sheets on small boats, though—they sometimes need to be cast off in a hurry, and undoing the half hitch is an extra step.

OTHER MATTERS
Sail bags. One especially helpful thing to do, if you are crewing for a friend, is to take proper care of the sails at the end of the day. The light sails—jibs, spinnakers, mizzen staysails and others—are usually bagged. This involves getting each one properly into a sail bag, with the tack (the lower, forward corner) at the top of the bag, so it's ready to fasten in place the next time you want to set the sail.

Once the sail is in the bag, tie a proper knot around the throat of the bag. Not just any knot, but a *miller's knot*, which you can figure out from the drawing on page 137. It is secure and yet can be easily untied.

The clove hitch can be used for lines that need to be adjusted, but it is greatly overrated.

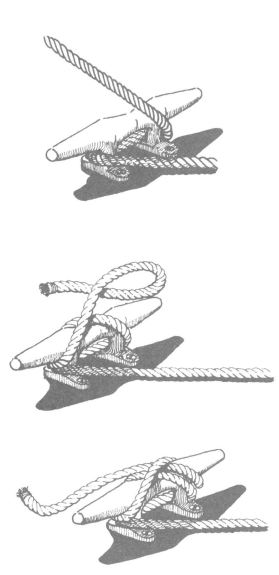

A correct lead to a cleat (left) is made at an angle, leaving the cleat free for the turns around it. An improper lead (right) tends to jam the first figure eight when you want to release the line.

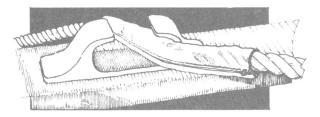

Lines that may chafe in chocks can be protected with chafing gear such as canvas sleeves.

The proper way to snub a line on a cleat is shown here. The friction of the dock line going around the cleat makes it easy to hold the boat securely. To fasten the snubbed line properly, make figure eights around the cleat, turning the last loop over so the free end is secured. Note: This final locking turn is not used for sheets, which must often be released quickly.

The right knife. If you don't have a knife yet, get one. It's the sailor's one indispensable tool. For most purposes, a pocketknife will do, but if you worry about losing it overboard, fasten a lanyard to the knife and to your belt. The standard folding rigging knife is a useful knife, with a strong, straight-edged blade, a marlinespike for separating the strands of a line that you plan to splice, and a special hasp that fits over shackle-bolt ends so that you can use it as you would a wrench.

Flemishing a line. If you have been around fancy yachts with professional crews, you have probably seen flat, circular coils of line on deck, beautifully *flemished*. To flemish a

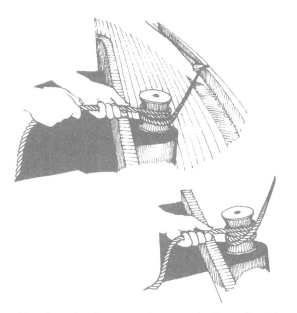

If a sheet leads properly to a winch and not too many turns are taken (left), the line won't bind in an override (right).

line, you coil it clockwise from the center out. A flemished coil is fine if the Grand Duchess is coming to visit or for other special occasions, but it's not for everyday use, and the coil will leave a dirty mark.

As mentioned earlier, the knots, bends, hitches, and splices illustrated are the basic ones, which will do for most practical situations. But as you become more proficient, you'll want to acquire one or two special tools for working with rope and one or more of the fascinating books about the art of ropework. Or, find a retired Coast Guard chief bos'n's mate who'll give you lessons in fancy work. That's an example of how one of the sailor's skills can become one of the sailor's arts.

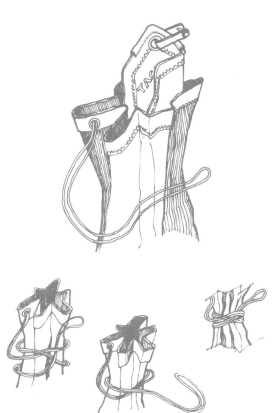

A miller's knot is used to secure a sail bag. Like most useful knots, it is tied quickly and can always be undone.

When you want to show off, a Flemish coil is a neat way to handle the end of a dockline. Used every day, it could mark the deck because it collects dirt.

THE LANGUAGE OF SAILING

The parts of a sailboat are described in Chapter 3; knots, bends, and hitches are explained in Chapter 9.

Abaft: When on board, astern of; i.e., the mizzenmast is abaft the mainmast.

Abeam: At right angles to the centerline of the boat, but not on the boat.

Accidental jibe: When the mainsail swings unexpectedly to the opposite side while a boat is sailing downwind; a potentially dangerous movement.

Aft: Near, or toward, the stern of the boat.

Alee: Away from the direction of the wind, usually referring to the movement of the helm or tiller.

Amidships: The center part of a vessel between bow and stern; also, that part of the vessel between the port and starboard sides.

Apparent wind: The wind that makes a boat sail; its strength and direction are those of the true wind as modified by the wind created by the boat's forward movement over the water (see *True wind*).

Astern: Opposite of *ahead*; behind a boat.

Athwartships: Across a boat from side to side.

Backing: The wind is said to be backing when it changes direction counterclockwise.

Backstay: Rigging that supports the mast from aft.

Backwind: Wind deflected by a boat's sail into the leeward side of another sail is said to backwind the sail.

Bail: A metal half-hoop used to hold a block to a boom.

Battens: Wood or plastic stiffeners placed in pockets in the leech of a sail to keep the edge from curling over.

Beam: The greatest width of a vessel.

Beam reach: Sailing with the apparent wind coming at right angles to the boat.

Bear down: Approach from windward.

Bear off: Change course and sail to leeward.

Bearing: The direction of an object relative to a boat, or as a true bearing as shown on a chart.

Beating: Sailing to windward in a series of tacks; sometimes used to mean simply sailing close-hauled or upwind (see *Point of sailing*).

Beaufort scale: A system of describing wind and sea conditions by number, from 0 for flat calm to 12 for a hurricane.

Before the wind: In the same direction as the wind is blowing.

Belay: Make fast a line to a cleat or belaying pin; also a verbal command to rescind a previous order or to stop an action being carried out.

Bend: A knot that fastens one line to another; also, as a verb, to attach a sail to a spar or stay.

Bight: Any part of a rope between the ends, but usually a loop.

Binnacle: A stand or case holding a boat's compass.

Block: The nautical word for pulley.

Board boat: A small sailboat with only one sail; the crew usually sits on the boat, rather than inside it.

Bolt rope: A line attached to and forming part of the foot or the luff of a sail to give it strength or to substitute for sail slides.

Boom: A spar to which the foot of a sail is attached. The boom itself is attached to a mast or to a stay.

Boom vang: A tackle running between boom and deck (or base of the mast) that flattens the sail's curve by a downward pull on the boom.

Boot top: The waterline stripe.

Bow: The forward part of a boat.

Bowsprit: A spar extending forward of the bow and set into the deck to support the headsails.

Broach: Swing out of control so that a boat is broadside to the wind and waves. Broaching can cause dangerous heeling and damage to rigging.

Broach reach: Sailing with the wind coming over either quarter of the boat.

By the lee: With the wind on the same side as the main boom while a boat is running; considered potentially dangerous because it invites an accidental jibe.

Burdened vessel: A vessel that, in accordance with right-of-way rules, is required to change course or speed to avoid collision with another vessel.

Cam cleat: A small spring-loaded device for holding lines under load.

Cast off: To unfasten a line; to unfasten all dock lines when leaving a dock.

Catamaran: A boat with twin parallel hulls.

Catboat: A sailboat with a single mast, stepped far forward, carrying one sail only (no headsails).

Centerboard: A plate or board that can be raised or lowered through a slot in the bottom of the boat. It provides lateral resistance against the water to prevent the boat from making leeway, or sideslipping.

Chafe: Wear on a sail, spar, or line caused by rubbing against something while in use. It can be prevented by chafing gear, which absorbs the friction.

Chain plate: A metal strap bolted to or molded in the side of a sailboat, to which a shroud or stay is attached.

Chock: A U-shaped fitting, usually metal, secured in or on a boat's rail, through which anchoring and mooring lines are led. An open fairlead.

Cleat: A double-horned fitting of wood or metal to which lines are secured, or *made fast*, or other devices (see *Cam cleat; Jam cleat*) that perform the same function.

Clew: The lower, after corner of a sail.

Close-hauled: A boat is said to be close-hauled when she is sailing as close as possible to the wind.

Close reach: Said of a boat when she is sailing with sheets eased but with the wind forward of the beam.

Cockpit: The area of a boat from which she is steered.

Cotter pin: A metal pin, doubled so the ends can be spread after it is inserted in a hole or slot; it is used to hold a metal fitting in place. A circular split ring is often used in place of a cotter pin.

Cringle: A ring sewn into a sail, through which a line may be passed.

Cunningham: A special cringle that is used with a line to alter and control the draft, or shape, of a mainsail.

Current: The horizontal movement of water, caused by the tide or wind, or both. (See *Tide.)*

Daggerboard: A type of removable centerboard that does not pivot but is raised and lowered vertically.

Displacement: The weight of water displaced by a floating vessel, hence, the weight of the vessel itself.

Downhaul: Tackle attached to the underside of a sliding gooseneck; it tightens the sail's luff by pulling down on the boom.

Draft: The depth of water at the lowest point of a vessel's keel.

Ease: Slacken; applies to sheets and other lines as well as to wind, weather, and current.

Eye of the wind: The direction from which the wind is coming.

Eye splice: A permanent loop in the end of a rope made by splicing, or weaving, the end of the rope back on itself.

Fairlead: A fitting that controls or changes the direction of a line.

Fall off: To allow a boat's bow to turn away from the wind.

Fathom: Six feet, usually seen as a measurement of depth on charts.

Fender: A cushion placed between boats or between a boat and a dock to prevent marring the hull.

Foot: The lower edge of a sail.

Forestay: A stay running from the mast down to the foredeck inside the jibstay on a vessel, such as a cutter, that carries more than one headsail. The forestaysail is hoisted on it.

Forward: Toward the bow.

Fouled: Tangled or caught; said of a line or an anchor.

Freeboard: The vertical distance from the waterline to the gunwale at its lowest point.

Gaff: A spar supporting the head of a four-sided fore-and-aft sail.

Gasket: A strip of Dacron or other material used for tying up the sails; also called a *stop*.

Genoa: A large jib that overlaps the mast.

Ghosting: A sailboat moving in little or no wind is said to be ghosting.

Gooseneck: The fitting that secures a boom to the mast; it can be fixed or can slide up and down.

Ground tackle: A collective term for the anchor and associated gear—cable, chain, swivel, etc.

Gudgeon and pintle: A socket and pin, by which a rudder is fastened to a boat.

Gunwale: The rail of a boat, i.e., the upper edge of a boat's hull; pronounced "gun'l."

Halyard: A line or wire used for hoisting sails.

Hank: A fitting for attaching a sail to a stay; a clip or snaphook.

"Hard alee": A command given to begin tacking, or coming about, accompanied by the action of pushing the tiller to leeward.

Head: The upper corner of a triangular sail. Also, the toilet facilities on a boat.

Headsails: Sails set forward of the foremost mast; includes jibs and staysails.

Head down; head off: To head away from the wind; the opposite of *head up*.

Head up: Steer a boat closer to the direction from which the wind is coming; the opposite of *head down* or *head off*.

Helm: The tiller or steering wheel; the steering apparatus and its effect.

Hitch: A method of making a rope fast to another rope or to a spar.

Heel: A vessel that leans to one side, as by wind pressure in the normal course of sailing, is said to heel.

In irons: A sailboat is said to be in irons when she is head to wind with no steerageway.

Jam cleat: A device with a V-shaped opening to hold a sheet or other line.

Jib: A triangular sail set forward of the foremost mast.

Jibe: Bring the wind to the opposite side of the boat when sailing downwind, so that the sails swing to the other side; the proper command is "Jibe ho!" (See also *Accidental jibe*.)

Jibsheet: The line that runs from the clew of the jib to the cockpit or deck, used to control the sail.

Jibstay: The forward stay on which the jib is hoisted.

Keel: The deepest part of a vessel, the structural section that protrudes beneath the main part of the hull. A keel boat has a permanent keel to prevent leeway, as opposed to a centerboard.

Ketch: A two-masted sailboat on which the mizzenmast (the aftermost mast) is shorter than the mainmast and is stepped forward of the rudder post.

Knockdown: The action and result when a boat is laid over suddenly by wind or sea, so that water pours over the gunwale.

Knot: A measure of speed equal to one nautical mile (6,076 feet) per hour.

Lay a mark: To be able to reach a mark, when

sailing close-hauled, without tacking. *Lay* also refers to the direction in which the strands of a rope are twisted.

Lead block: A pulley used to control a guy or sheet; the lead block is often a snatch block (see *Snatch block*).

Leech: The after, or rear, edge of a sail.

Leeward: The direction away from that in which the wind is blowing; pronounced "lu'ard."

Leeway: The drift a boat makes to leeward when she is sailing at an angle to the wind.

Lee helm: The tendency of a boat under sail to turn away from the wind when the helm is amidships. (See also *Weather helm*.)

Lift: A rigging line used to control or hold a boom or spinnaker pole.

List: The leaning of a vessel to one side due to uneven distribution of weight.

Loose-footed: Said of a sail that is secured to the boom at the tack and clew only.

Lubber line: A mark inside the compass, representing a boat's heading.

Luff: As a noun, the forward edge of a sail; as a verb, to head a boat up into the wind, thus causing the sail to flutter; the fluttering of the sail is called luffing.

Mainmast: The tallest mast on a boat.

Mainsail: The sail set abaft the mainmast; pronounced "mains'l."

Mainsheet: The line controlling the mainsail.

Marlinespike: A tool for opening the strands of a rope or wire while splicing it.

Mast step: The strong brace or fitting on which the bottom of a mast rests.

Mizzen: The after and smaller mast of a ketch or yawl; also, the sail set on that mast.

Mooring: A place to tie a boat up to, usually a semipermanent anchor and gear (chain, float, pendant, swivel) left in place in the water.

Off the wind: Sailing with the wind abeam or astern.

Outhaul: A device on the boom for stretching the foot of the sail out along the boom from the mast.

Overhaul: Remove kinks and snarls from a line.

Pendant: A control line for a pivoting centerboard or a movable rudder blade; the rope portion of a permanent mooring attached to the pick-up buoy or float. Pronounced "pennant."

Pennant: A small flag, often used to indicate wind direction.

Painter: Dinghy towrope or dockline.

Pinching: Sailing a boat closer to the wind than she can efficiently go.

Pintle: See *Gudgeon*.

Pointing: Sailing close to the wind.

Point of sailing: The direction of the boat in relation to the wind: beating, reaching, or running (see individual terms).

Port: The left side of a vessel, looking forward, or the direction to the left.

Port tack: Sailing with the wind coming over a boat's port side.

Privileged vessel: One that has the right of way.

Pulpit: An elevated tubular metal guardrail at the bow or stern.

Quarter: Either side of a boat, from the stern to amidships.

Rake: The angle of a vessel's mast from the perpendicular; a mast usually rakes aft.

Reach: The point of sailing between close-hauled and running, with the wind abeam.

"Ready about": The order given to alert the crew before tacking. (The next order is "Hard alee.")

Reef: Reduce the area of the sail.

Reef points: Short lines set in rows along the sail, used for reefing.

Reeve: The extra area in the curved leech of a sail; beyond a straight line from head to clew.

Rigging screw: See *Turnbuckle*.

Roach: The extra area in the curved leech of a sail; beyond a straight line from head to clew.

Rode: Anchor line.

Roller furling: A method of rolling a jib up on its stay.

Roller reefing: A method of reefing the mainsail in which the sail is wound up by rotating the boom.

Running: Sailing with the wind astern.

Running rigging: Sheets, halyards, guys, lifts and other frequently adjusted lines.

Schooner: A vessel with two or more masts carrying fore-and-aft sails. If two-masted, the foremast is shorter than the mainmast.

Scope: The ratio of length of anchor line used to depth of water; expressed as "5 to 1," etc.

Secure: Make fast.

Seize: Bind with a thin line.

Shackle: A metal link, usually U-shaped, with a pin that unscrews to open the shackle so that it can be attached to a line, a sail, or a fitting; a snap shackle has a spring-loaded pin that unlocks to open the shackle.

Sheave: The wheel inside a block or at the mast head or mast foot, on which a line turns; pronounced: "shiv".

Sheet: A line used to trim a sail.

Shock cord: Strong elastic line used for special rigging purposes such as keeping a topping lift out of the way of a sail.

Shroud: Standing rigging that supports a mast at the sides.

Sloop: A single-masted sailboat whose principal sails are a main and a jib.

Snatch block: A block that opens at the side so that a line can be hooked into it without reeving the entire line.

Spars: A general term for masts, booms, poles, gaffs, etc., that hold sails extended.

Spinnaker: A light headsail used in running and reaching, and shaped a bit like a parachute.

Splice: Join two ropes permanently by weaving their strands together alternately over and under each other.

Spreaders: Bars fastened aloft on a mast to increase the angle of the shrouds.

Spring line: A long dock line that prevents movement, forward or aft, of a docked boat.

Standing part: The fixed part of a rope or line that takes the strain, as opposed to the free ends or the bight.

Standing rigging: The shrouds and stays supporting the mast.

Starboard: The right side of the vessel, facing forward, or the direction to the right.

Stay: Rigging supporting the mast from forward or aft.

Staysail: Any of various fore-and-aft sails, usually triangular but sometimes quadrilateral, generally set in addition to or inside the boat's other sails, e.g., forestaysail, spinnaker staysail, mizzen staysail, fisherman staysail; pronounced: "stays'l".

Steerageway: A boat has steerageway when she is moving through the water with enough speed so that the rudder can control and change her direction.

Stern: The back of a boat.

Stops: Tape, sewn cloth strips, or short pieces of line used to hold a sail in place after it is furled.

Tack: As a noun, the lower forward corner of a sail; the way in which a boat is moving with respect to the wind, i.e., a boat is on a port or starboard tack depending on which side the wind is from. As a verb, to come about, or turn the bow of the boat through the eye of the wind.

Tacking: Changing tacks, or coming about; sailing upwind on a zigzag course so that the boat is alternately on a port and a starboard tack.

Tackle: Ropes and blocks rigged together for hauling; pronounced "tayk'l."

Tang: A fitting, usually on the upper part of a mast, to which a stay or shroud is made fast.

Telltale: A wind-direction indictor made of cloth, yarn or feather, fastened to a shroud or sail.

Thwart: A seat extending across a boat.

Tide: The vertical movement of water caused by the gravitational pull of the sun and moon. (See also *Current.*)

Tiller: The long lever by which the rudder is moved.

Topping lift: An adjustable line from the masthead to the end of the boom; used to hold up the boom when the sail is not set. Also called a *boom lift.*

True wind: The actual direction and speed of the wind, as opposed to the apparent direction and speed. (See also *Apparent wind.*)

Turnbuckle or *rigging screw*: A mechanical device for adjusting the tension on stays and shrouds.

Vang: See *Boom vang.*

Veering: Wind veers when its direction changes in a clockwise direction.

Warp: Move or turn a boat around a dock or pilings, using dock lines and spring lines.

Weather helm: The tendency of a boat, with its rudder amidships, to turn by itself to windward. (See also *Lee helm.*)

Weather side: The upwind side.

Whipping: A binding of light line or tape on the end of a line to keep it from fraying.

Winch: A drum-shaped device around which a line is coiled; it provides mechanical advantage when a line is being brought in under load.

Windward: The general direction from which the wind is coming; pronounced "wind'ard."

Wing and wing: A boat is said to be sailing wing and wing when she is sailing downwind with the mainsail and jib set and filled on opposite sides of the boat.

Yawl: A two-masted vessel whose mizzen is small and stepped abaft the rudder post.

REQUIRED ON-BOARD EQUIPMENT

All boats must carry readily accessible personal flotation devices (PFDs) for each person on board. In addition, all boats must be able to make sound signals, although the requirements for bells, whistles, and horns vary with the size of the vessel. Visual signaling devices, which vary in type relative to daytime and nightime usage, are also required.

Any boat with an inboard engine or any boat with enclosed cabin space and an outboard motor must have one or more fire extinguishers, the number and type of which depend on the size and the usage of the boat.

Navigation lights are also imperative; the type necessary varies with the size and type of boat. A very small sailboat must carry at least a flashlight.

Full information on the required types of lights, fire extinguishers, and PFDs for each size and type of pleasure boat is given in Chapman's *Piloting, Seamanship & Small Boat Handling.* Many other important items of equipment—anchors, compasses, dock lines, charts, and flashlights—are not specified by law because their usage varies.

INDEX